LEARNING ORGANIZATION DEVELOPMENT STRATEGIES

JOHN LOK

Contents

Foreword

Preface

This book concerns how to apply how behavioral economic and psychological methods to attempt to explain whether your organization can be influenced to raise your employee individual productive efficiency as well as improve service performance to achieve to let your clients feel more satisfaction by effective human resource training or/and facility management methods. My research questions include: Can effective human resource training or/and facility management influences your organization's employee individual productive efficiency raising and/or service performance improving?

Can effective workplace working environment facility management influence your organization's employee individual emotion and working attitude to be changed more positive to raise productive efficiency and/or service performance? Can effective human resource training program improve your organization's employee individual skill level in order to raise productive efficiency and/or service performance? Has it relationship between effective human resource training and facility management to influence organization's employee individual productive efficient level and service performance in long term? I shall apply psychological method to attempt to recommend whether it is the right time to your organization ought need to find methods to raise your organization's human resource trai8ning course(s) quality and/or improve your organization's facility management in-house service quality to let your employees feel more comfortable to work in your organization's any working environment in order to achieve the raising productive efficiency and/or improving service performance consequence in possible.

This book divides five parts. The first part indicates how organizations can attempt to apply different psychological methods to research how and why employee individual selects to do the behavioral performance in organizations in order to let any organization leaders can judge whether it is right time that whose organization ought need to attempt to change human resource training courses quality in order to let employees' skills can be improved more effectively and/or applying facility management to be implemented more comfortable to let employees to feel in order to achieve the productive efficient raising and/or the service performance improving possible consequence in long term.

The second part indicates to explain whether effective human resource training courses can help to raise employee productive efficiency and/or improve service performance. I shall indicate the whole HRM successful elements to explain whether it can still help the organization to raise employee efficiency and/or improve service performance, if the organization neglects to implement an effective human resource training course program to let whose employees to attempt to learn any work-related skills.

The second part concerns challenge of HR management it is as a HR specialist, what are the challenges you may face and what HR intervention mechanisms would you consider using in an attempt to drive individual and organization performance in a multinational company? Critically evaluate this question by utilizing the appropriate academic literatures.

This part explains why human resource strategy can bring organizational benefits. It will explain how reward strategy can bring what kinds of benefits to organizations. Reward management is nowadays considered as an important topic in order to achieve the goals of a company. Employees are considered as the main factor which plays an important role in the organization. The success of each and every organization is its dedicated employee's .Current world is filled with changes and competition. In order to survive in the current situation companies should be having employees who are loyal and expert in their own field. New technologies are developed constantly and the companies are eagerly trying to catch up those talented employees with right expertise in their own areas. So, fair award management can attract talented employees to choose the organization to work.

The final part indicates whether organization's facility management in-house department or outsourced department can achieve to improve its office or warehouse working environment to be more comfortable to let employees to feel in order to influence their productive efficiencies to be raised or improving their service performance to bring customers' more satisfactory feeling.

I write this book aims to hope any organization leaders can attempt to apply psychological methods to predict whether their in-house facility management service is enough or/and human resource management strategy and training course program strategies which both have relationship to influence their employees' productive efficiency and service performance in order to achieve aim to raise more satisfactory feeling to their customers. I believe that effective facility management can improve better workplace environment to influence employee individual productive efficiency raising as well as effective human resource training course program can improve employee individual service performance in order to achieve customers to feel more satisfactory service performance in consequence for the organization's service.

In the final part, I will explain how any why effective department communication, excellent technological input, effective human resource developement training, good employee motivation strategy and effective performance measurement strategy can influence any organization's overall performance to be more effective. I shall indicate the reasons to explain why above any one of these factors have indirect relationship to influence the organization's overall performance effectiveness. Readers can earn fresh opinions to acknowledge that these any one factors can be possible to influence organization's overall performance effectiveness.

Prologue

Table of contents

CHAPTER ONE

REWARD MANAGEMENT STRATEGY

What is reward management strategy?

1. Can effective human resource training or/and facility management influences your organization's employee individual productive efficiency raising and/or service performance improving?
2. Can effective workplace working environment facility management influence your organization's employee individual emotion and working attitude to be changed more positive to raise productive efficiency and/or service performance?
3. Can effective human resource training program improve your organization's employee individual skill level in order to raise productive efficiency and/or service performance?
4. Has it relationship between effective human resource training and facility management to influence organization's employee individual productive efficient level and service performance in long term?

I shall apply psychological method to attempt to recommend whether it is the right time to your organization ought need to find methods to raise your organization's human resource trai8ning course(s) quality and/or improve your organization's facility management in-house service quality to let your employees feel more comfortable to work in your organization's any working environment in order to achieve the raising productive efficiency and/or improving service performance consequence in possible.

Why does organizations need reward management strategy that is concerned with the formulation and implementation of strategies and policies that aim to reward people fairly, equitably and consistently in accordance with their value to the organization. Reward management consists of analyzing and controlling employee remuneration, compensation and all of the other benefits for the employees. Reward management aims to create and efficiently operate a reward structure for an organization. Reward structure usually consists of pay policy and practices, salary and payroll administration, total reward, minimum wage, executive pay and team reward.

Reward is the generic term for the totality of financial and non-financial compensation or total remuneration paid to an employee in return for work or service rendered at work. Reward, which is sometimes been refer to as compensation or remuneration, is perhaps the most important contract term in every paid-employment. Its impact on workers (or employee's) performance is in most instance greatly misinterpreted. The understanding of this term is very important; this is because the incentive scheme given to an employee will influence the behavior and level of engagement to the organization. However, basic pay, it is a straightforward payment scheme which may not provide incentives to individual workers because they are not based on output or performance. This pay is often in relation to a given period like an hourly rate, weekly wage or annual salary. It's also an established rate for all workers in one category. Incentive for group, Plant/enterprise-based it is refer to as grain sharing within large group or the whole organization. This pay scheme is use in organizations where the workforce can clearly see the results of their efforts. Award can include two kinds. Intrinsic reward include- Achievement, feeling of accomplishment, recognition, job satisfaction, personal growth and status, job enlargement, job enrichment, team working, empowerment. Otherwise, extrinsic rewards also include formal-recognition; base wage or salary, incentive payments, fringe benefits, promotion, social relationship and work environment. This study will explain and define different type of pay and non-financial scheme use in today's organizations.

Reward Management is concerned with the formulation and implementation of strategies and policies that aim to reward people fairly, equitably and consistently in accordance with their value to the organization. Reward management forms the organization relationship. This if an HR manager is to succeed in successfully managing the employment relationship, he/she will have to do well in reward management, otherwise these will be an in balance in the employment relationship, such as strikes, lockouts. Objectives of Reward Management may include: Support the organization's strategy, recruit & retain, motivate employees, internal & external equity, strengthen psychological contract, financially sustainable, comply with legislation and efficiently administered.

Basic Types of Reward include

- Extrinsic rewards

– satisfy basic needs: survival, security

– Pay, conditions, treatment

- Intrinsic rewards

– satisfy higher needs: esteem, development

Rewards by Individual, Team, Organization

- Individual: base pay, incentives, benefits

– rewards attendance, performance, competence

- Team

– team bonus, rewards group cooperation

- Organization

– profit-sharing, shares, gain-sharing

In general , a profitable reward management system should have these characteristics: Simplicity must be easily understood by everyone in the organization. People must understand why they are getting, what they are getting from the employment relationship . Fairness and equitability, every component of the system must be justifiable and consistently applied. But reward management has related problems, such as strike, staff turnover, dissatisfaction etc. An effective participatory reward management system should be negotiated and agreed better management and employees.

What is the role of Compensation and Reward in Organization? Compensation and Reward system plays vital role in a business organization. Since, among four Ms, i.e. Men, Material, Machine and Money, Men has been most important factor, it is impossible to imagine a business process without Men. Land, Labor, Capital and Organization are four major factors of production.

Every factor contributes to the process of production/business. It expects return from the business process such as rent is the return expected by the Landlord. Similarly Capitalist expects interest and organizers i.e. Entrepreneur expects profits. The labor expects wages from the process. It is evident that other factors are in-human factors and as such labor plays vital role in bringing about the process of production/business in motion. The other factors being human, has expectations, emotions, ambitions and egos. Labor therefore expects to have fair share in the business/ production process.

What are the advantages of Fair Compensation System?

Therefore a fair compensation system is a must for every business organization. The fair compensation system will help in the following:

- If an ideal compensation system is designed, it will have positive impact on the efficiency and results produced by workmen.
- Such system will encourage the normal worker to perform better and achieve the standards fixed.
- This system will encourage the process of job evaluation. It will also help in setting up an ideal job evaluation, which will have transparency, and the standards fixing would be more realistic and achievable.
- Such a system would be well defined and uniform. It will be apply to all the levels of the organization as a general system.
- The system would be simple and flexible so that every worker/recipient would be able to compute his own compensation receivable.
- Such system would be easy to implement, so that it would not penalize the workers for the reasons beyond their control and would not result in exploitation of workers.
- It will raise the morale, efficiency and cooperation among the workers. It, being just and fair would provide satisfaction to the workers.
- Such system would help management in complying with the various labor acts.
- Such system would also bring about amicable settlement of disputes between the workmen union and management.

● The system would embody itself the principle of equal work equal wages. Encouragement for those who perform better and opportunities for those who wish to excel.

Factors affect an organization's reward policy and strategy which include: affordability, it means what an organization can afford to pay the argument is that an organization can't borrow to reward employees, but should reward from the value created by the employees themselves. However, an organization has to afford to pay above legal minimums, legislation sets the minimum base pay (minimum fixed pay rates), which becomes the starting point in calculating for all of an organization's policies. Workers committees/trade unions depend on the power of a union, pay levels are determined through collective bargaining. The most powerful ones will strike higher levels, external job value means the market value of the job, e.g. what is the market value or HR manager or clerical assistant? Internal job value means the value or perceived value of a job compared to other jobs which the organization will determine the reward that job, e.g. HR manager compared to finance manager. Value of the person means employees holding similar jobs can be paid differently depending on the value of the organization performance and the economy environment influence means (labor supply/demand). Some authors explained a depressed economy increased the supply of labor, which reduced its price and have effect reward policy strategy.

Thus, reward system strategy means a benefit plan management procedure and it needs to implement these steps in order to achieve its fair reward as below:

Step one, deciding objective to assess what the company wants to achieve through its benefit strategy and policy, and its ability to pay for the changes;

Step two, obtaining view points and input from employees to collect employees‘ view points through employee surveys, focus groups and individual interviews;

Step third, analyzing competitiveness to establish or determine the company's competitive position, though conducting a customized survey or collecting available market data from external providers;

Step fourth, designing the benefit package to determine the mix and scale of the benefit package, the allocation of benefit, the scope for flexibility and the cost of benefit provision;

Step fifth, consulting the senior management team and employees on the proposal to get input and buy in from senior management team to make amendments if necessary, collecting comments and effort the non-financial rewards as benefits; step sixth, planning the communication to inform everyone concerned what is happening, why it is happening and how it affects them,

The final step , evaluation to review the plan on a regular basis and obtain input from employees and management for evaluation purposes.

Strategy reward system pay for perform two elements: Financial reward includes base salary, pay incentives, employee benefits. Non-financial reward includes intrinsic rewards, centers in the work itself, praise, recognition , time off. Reward system is a key driver of-HR strategy, business strategy organization culture strategic reward system related to HR system. Such as skill-based pay to training, overtime pay rules to labor relations, sign-on bonus to employment, merit pay to performance management and merit pay to performance culture.

Thus one successful reward strategy system will have these characteristics. Performance and reward strategy, identify requirement and develop strategy, analyze data and performance and reward information on individuals or group and achieve colleges to aid decision making, work with managers to certain and develop reward requirements for key individuals within their area, review and analyze the organization strategy demographic profile and market activity against current reward activity to identify current reward activity to identify current and long term reward requirement to assess internal and external factors driving reward requirements against plan. Explain to employees how pay and reward fits and supports overall people processes and activities, such as performance management.

In conclusion, what is award's aim ? For the organisation, reward should aim at; recruiting the quantity and quality required, encourage suitable staff to be loyal and remain in the organisation, provide rewards for good performance and incentives for further improvement in performance, maintain appropriate differentials relative to values of different levels of job, the reward adopted by organisation should be flexible enough to accommodate changes in the market rate for different skills and should be cost effective. For individual employees the reward system should be fair and equitable in valuation of the worth in comparison with others. The third which is the union of employees, the system should ensure maximum benefits for members without undue prejudices to their future security by making their reward to pace with the cost of living and the prosperity of the organisation.

What kinds of benefits of reward strategy which can bring to organizations? Good employee benefits and services can help the organization by reducing potential employee discontent, satisfying their needs and discouraging labor unrest or raising labor turnover. Thus, with competitive benefit programs , an organization can be more effective in recruitment and employee retention, thus reducing labor turnover.

Employee benefits may include legally required payments, such as workers compensation, long service pay or retirement payment, sickness allowance and end of year payment, bonus as well as optional welfare plans, such as life insurance, medical/hospital /dental coverage to self and family' education allowance, housing allowance, quarters, subsidized loans, retirement, pension plan, meal allowance, travelling allowance, paid time off, pay sick leave, other special paid leave, five day week, paid annual leave and maternity leave.

Employee service mean the organizations can choose to provide various services ranging from work related to those satisfying personal or family needs, in order to encourage employees to work happily and stay with a particular organization. The service may include social functions or recreational activities, e.g. New Year dinner, annual ball, company picnics, free transportation service, food service or canteen ,purchase of used equipment no longer required by the company, credit unions, low-interest loans, legal services, child care and elder care services, free holiday apartment, air ticket allowance etc. employees' welfares.

1.1 Why does organization need reward management system?

Some HR professionals feel reward management can earn these benefits to organizations. In compensation and benefits reward management aspect, it is not possible to imagine an offer of employment that does not indicate a salary or wage and possibly other terms of compensation as well as description of the various benefits available with the employment. So, a candidate accepts or rejects the job offer, he/she will regard how a compensation package with a monetary of non-monetary value, such as a fair exchange for whose labor. So, the award management plan will include monetary reward and non-monetary reward both is better than monetary reward only. For example, piece rate pay is good for factory workers, commissions have long been a major part of the compensation of salespeople and merit pay and bonuses are well established methods of rewarding good performance for car salespeople. So, the variable or incentive pay is a good reward implementation plan for salespeople, insurance agents.

How to evaluate the base pay level is the more accurate? Leon, M. (2002) indicated that when a company needs to determine levels of base pay, the best companies have several objectives. The most important , in a global business environment characterized by strong demand for talented experienced employees is to be competitive. The determination of base pay level does not depend on only in one's own industry, but also in other industries competing for the same talent. In fact, a firm's closes competition for human resources often is not its closet industrial competitor. In addition, the best companies are attractive to the levels of compensation appropriate to the different regions and countries where facilities are located or where workers originate. At the same time, some are developing truly global talent managers, whose pay scales are most pay level to similar manager in other companies than they are with typical rate of pay in either the firm's headquarter country or its overseas locations.

Is one company achieves higher profits, it needs to raise higher wage to its all employees? I feel that it depends on whether situations to make decisions to raise all employees' wages , due to it has higher profit reason in the year.

Robert, P.V. (2006) summarized these rules in dealing with subordinates, their performance should be enhanced. These rules includes using fair differential rewarding, it means that many managers try to treat all subordinates alike. When all employees receive equal rewards, superior performers begin to feel that their efforts are unappreciated, when poorer recognize that they won't be penalized for minimal effort. In response, over time, most above-average performers will drop their performance to the minimal level.

A few superior performers may persist absolutely , but most will lower their efforts to the level that they feel equals their rewards. So, when rewards are commensurate with performance, however, subordinates receive a quite different message. Superior performers get the signal that their efforts are valued, and potentially high performers are encouraged to try harder, identifying valued rewards for individual , it means that if a manager hopes to influence an employee's behavior through the use of rewards, the rewards must have value to the employee. One of the best ways to obtain such information is simply to ask employees what rewards they could like to receive. Younger workers may prefer more paid vacation days, (non-monetary value reward) or greater participation in decision making (high position management role) . The older workers may choose better medical insurance or a longer contribution to their pension plan, instructing subordinated on how rewards are tied to performance. It means that in order for maximizing organization's effectiveness, employees must clearly understand how rewards and performance are connected. When specific information is lacking, subordinates may try to second-guess their manager's intentions by constructing their own imagined system of rewards. Thus, much under productivity can be avoid of a manager clearly states goals for performance and explains how rewards will be related to performance, providing information feedback on performance means that in order to meet their manager's standards of performance, employees must have instructive feedback. Their manager must evaluate their information for them, indicating how well or how poorly they are doing and suggesting specific ways to improve. In addition to providing guidance, feedback can also serve as an additional form of suggestion.

Thus, when an organization earns higher profit, it seems that it ought not raise all employees salaries to be higher, because some hard working employees will feel unfair if the lazy employees can raise the same salary level to same to the hard working employees in the year. On the consequence, the hard working employees will be possible to under productivity or productivity in below level efficiency or inefficiency to perform their unsatisfactory or disagreed feeling to complain whose employers. Then, the organization will encounter low productivity in possible. Hence, fair reward management plan to all employees which is needed in any organization.

1.1.1 Why do IT and bank and property management and school organizations need reward management system?

In IT and bank and property industries which need reward strategic reasons: Reward management systems have major impact on organization capability to catch, retain and motivate high potential employees and as a result getting the high level of performance. I also believe reward of employee performance can lead tc differentiation between the productivity of the bank employees. In fact, bank employee performance is originally what on employee does or does not do. Performance of employees could include quantity of output, quality of output, timeliness of output, presence at work, cooperativeness.

Reward management in bank service industry, bank organization needs have effective and attractive reward management system to attract talent human resource applications. But banks are facing global saving bank competition. Reward management system is a core function of human resource discipline and is a strategic partner with company management. An good reward management can raise bank service employees performance in loan, saving mortgage etc. different departments. An effective reward management system can shorten service timeliness to raise talent employee individual bank service performance, raise the talent employee team cooperative effort in loan, mortgage, counter etc. different service departments.

However, reward management system tool includes both financial and non-financial rewards which are also called as extrinsic and intrinsic rewards. In bank industry financial rewards include salary increase, bonus, commission, housing loan allowance, education loan allowance. The non-financial rewards include promotion and title, authority and responsibility, appreciation and praise, participation to decisions, vacation time, comfort of working place, social authority, customer and management positive oral and written feedback, flexible working hours, design of work recognition , social rights, etc.

Property management industry reward management practitioners include property managers, caretakers, attendants, security guards, facility maintenance workers and cleaners. It is essential for employers to formulate strategic plans and coordinate labor relations of human resource with the development. In responds to the people-related challenge and opportunities to property management industry. It includes six aspects: communicating and improving staff benefits, promoting work-life balance and health and enhancing work arrangements, enhancing staff's career development and promotion prospect, improving the professional image of the industry, friendly employment practices for mature persons. Through these practices enterprises can make their job vacancies about attractive and answer misunderstandings about the property management industry.

Thus, the manpower shortage challenge will be avoid , when the people have interest to join the industry and they feel the reward is attractive to them to develop career. How to improve staff benefit? It includes new recruit entry bonus schemes, giving out little gifts and bonuses, during celebrations and festive occasions, and granting gratuities to critically ill employees or on the death of the employee's immediate family members, offers employees insurance plans, offering award schemes for employee's children by granting scholarships to outstanding students in recognition of their excellent exchange scholarships are available to subsidize their children's study abroad, promoting working-life balance to staff, such as organizing interest classes, setting up sports teams, organizing gatherings, participating in charitable activities, encouraging employees to organize social gatherings, promoting happiness at work, strengthening occupational safety and health arrangements to employees, e.g. setting up occupational safety and health committee / departments, formulating occupational safety and health policies, entertainment of work arrangement: compressed working days, five-day work week, flexible working days, flexible rostering, job sharing, part time work pattern, most rest time for frontline employee, job nature or workflow modification / re-engineering, improvement of employee's workplace environment, intra-district redeployment.

Reward is an important element in information technology industry. The IT industry had been needing a leader in changing traditional compensation strategy. Pay for performance needs to be designed effective reward system to encourage IT employee to work hardly in order to reward and contribute the most to an IT organization's technological productivity and profits.

The compensation mix depends on deliverable and the impact it has on the IT business. Consequently higher the responsibility greater the variable content in the pay package. IT industry has many IT professionals , such as programmers, software or hardware engineers, e-commerce website designer etc. different IT professionals. Hence, different IT professionals need have different skills to evaluate pay performance level fairly. However, performance related pay plans, it is a motivator the improves productivity. It helps in improving IT product productivity and performance levels when making every IT professional individual equally to encourage or motivate them to work to hardly in their IT unique professional aspects. It is a greater motivator for top performances and teams as they can get fair and reasonable reward and pay according to their contributions.

In fact, there is no standard formula for a performance -related incentive plan, it is unique for each IT professional. However, the incentive plan should need to be design to each IT professional with an organization's objectives. They include, communication and understanding of objectives, consideration of different IT professional performance against objectives, translating evaluation into the kid of IT professional performance rating, a link between ratings and pay to the kind of IT unique professional skill.

University HR strategic reward management system(review promote monitor scheme) aims to improve systems and skills for teaching employee communication, support teaching management to play a move active role in communication key messages, ensure school reward policies and procedures are fair to teaching staffs and administrative non-teaching staffs in salary rank increasing level, establish improved consultation procedures at academic and teaching service level, demonstrate the values and ethics by the university through management practices and communication with teaching staffs and non-teaching staffs, improve the profile and performance of the university by recruiting and developing talent teaching employees with appropriate external recognition , certain academic disciplines present more different recruitment challenges and profile of the university as an employer could be improved in the academic labour market, recruiting sample of selection decisions through early stages of employment to assess quality of appointment and identify learning points, support and encourage recruitment messages to improve selection practice including skills and high quality appointment decisions, raise the profile of the university as an employer regionally, nationally and internationally, establish succession planning for all key roles and positions linked with clear career progression with job families, to face in a difficult economic climate the university needs to continue to attract and keep high quality staff to work in an efficient and cost effective manner. The extension of workload allocation models to all academic units is an important tool to assist in managing workload fairly and more effectively, well targeted and designed training and development is very effective in motivating and enabling staff and support productivity.

1.1.2 Why do small organizations need reward strategy?

Reward strategy can be applied to large organization, it can be also applied to small organization, e.g. family business, family business also needs compensation policies, the result encourages professional growth among family members and other employees as well as strategic business goal accomplishment. In general, compensation can be divided into the categories of base pay (equity as a basic for fairness , benefit, e.g. health care insurance, salary , wages, incentive compensation (e.g. bonuses, deferred compensation, stock or share options) and perks e.g. club membership, use of the company's private mountain, beach for holiday entertainment or sport activities e.g. free golf sport and company 's automobiles to provide to employees to drive in their private time.

Craig, E. A (2011) indicated that although small business has less employees , but it also needs compensation adjustments. The reasons include: (1) performance-based increases i.e. a rise, (2) annual wage adjustments e.g. cost of living increases to remain with what comparable businesses are paying and corrective adjustments to more pay for a position into with other position in the business increases are considered to be a key component of compensation by managers and non-management employers alike. The difference between one small organization's and one large organization's performance based increase is possible that one large organization has more a rise amount of performance -based increases in every time performance review. Otherwise, one small organization has less a rise amount of performance -based increases in every time performance review.

A good reward strategy can develop a philosophy of compensation that builds a framework for base pay and incentive tailored to the special values, goals, and needs of the particular family firm. Hence, one family or small firm's compensation -reward strategy can be explained to be needed, due to these factors : the firm can compare pay and performance levels with those of businesses with whom which compete for employees, the firm's goal is to provide total compensation between median and the percentage of comparable groups, base salary will be made more accurate decision at or high or below the median level for the comparable groups, individual salaries will be made more accurate decision within how much percent of the midpoint for the firm's comparison group's salary range, the firm can make more accurate decision on emphasizing whether performance -based incentives ought be spent at the expense of the salary, whether annual incentives ought be exceed those of comparably sized competitors, whether long-term incentives ought be based on results that add shareholder value.

However, culture can influence some business owners how to make compensation issues, culture means beliefs, values, assumption, habits and behavior patterns of the organization. The reasons staffs are paid the way, they are may be partly unconscious and may arise from the personal and family history and the deeply felt personal needs of the business leader or leaders. So, any family or small business will ought try to develop a philosophy of compensation (reward) strategy , which may learn a great deal about itself in the process. For example, a entrepreneur has confidence in her or his ability to manage compensation on a case-by-case basis and maintain tight personal tight personal control over each individual pay, perks, incentives, dividends, and gifts in order to encourage its employees can raise more effort to increase the sale number to its different kinds of product in its shop. Otherwise, if a family member working in this kind of culture asks for a raise, the business owner will not talk to about how to raise compensation to his/her salespeople in Christmas period. Hence , culture seems to influence the large organization and small organization how to make itself compensation to salespeople in Christmas period.

However, a basis for fairness to base pay which can let the large organization or small organization's staffs to feel, it is very important , when the large or small organization needs to focus on filling a vacancy and getting new skills into key areas quickly to meet customer needs with quality and efficiency. Because if the large organization or small organization expects it sale turnover may increase or staff turnover may decrease, but hiring needed talent may become more difficult, indicating that the company's pay structure may have lost internal logic if it's basic pay is unfair to attract talent staffs choose to join to its organization to work, when they feel that the organization's base pay is not reasonable to compare its competitors (pay for one job compared to another), and comparable jobs outside the company, the process is logical , objective and fair to be needed to judge the base pay structure to any organizations. Having a consistent, explainable ration for how compensation or reward is critical for employee and shareholders judgements about fairness. Hence, individual employee will usually compare his/her job in the company's salary and his/her similar job in another company's salary whether whose salary is same or more or less between whose company salary and similar company salary. Hence, a company needs to establish equitable base pay in a market value and merit system, with any adjustments , pay raises being a function of performance merit in order to make more reasonable compensation or reward to let its staffs to feel to avoid staff turnover number raises.

A rational compensation system steps can include: creating job description for all jobs, conducting a job evaluation to rank order jobs and determining which jobs that are similar in their importance to the business, obtaining external wage and salary survey information for representation jobs, utilizing other sources for comparable external data when needed, determining the company's reward strategy for compensation and deciding whether it wants pay to be set at the market average , whether it wants compensation at levels above or below the market average, or whether it wants to make a culture statement with pay levels, creating a wage and salary structure of starting pay levels, (minimums) and levels of pay for the most experienced workers (maximums). Analyzing current pay levels against the new structure pay levels against the new structure to determine which jobs are paid appropriately and which ones are not, considering individual, unique jobs that may have qualitative more or less important than external market comparable might suggest, making pay adjustments for those that are not of the range, accelerating regular increases for positions below the target range and decelerating or not making increased that are above the range. Finally , it needs to periodical check or review the wage and salary structure against outside bench market (external similar competitors positions to maintain external equity).

The point factor job evaluation tool can help the organization to make decision whether the staff ought pay how much salary level is the most reasonable. The point method include the elements such as : The experience element means the factor appraises the length of time normally required for an individual to acquire the necessary knowledge and ability to affectively perform the duties of the job. The experience level element means that whether the worker individual working experience in the firm, e.g. up to three months, he/she can earn the lowest points, till to comprehensive over right years, he/she can earn the highest points. The direction of others element means this factor appraises the responsibility to the job , it includes for organization, selection , assignment , guidance and review of personnel and the performance of other supervisory tasks. The direction of others level can indicate the employee earns none points when whose jobs involves no responsibility or authority for the direction of others, till to the highest points when the employee can confirm to own administrative ability,whose job is responsible for general administrative or executive supervision of all or broad segment of company operations as well as he/she can establish general policies and procedures and formulates and applies broad plans of operations.

Compensation specialists can help the company to select representative jobs from a company and find good external comparisons. They will need to make adjustment. Some criteria for determining a jobs‘ market value can include position title and job description, industry, size of company, sales or revenue volume, cost of living, based on location etc. data to determine whether their company's salary level is acceptable or reasonable to a job's market value. They need to gather the data concerns the job's market value. This is helpful because the latest supply and demand factors can affect certain positions may not show up in surveys. They must need to gather similar industry's organization size, sale or revenue volume data, daily cost of living and transportation cost how to influence their employees' income and similar competitors‘ employees income in order to make more reasonable and accurate salary structure adjustment.

1.2 Reward management aims to bring positive influence to work performance, how to achieve high work performance?

How can reward management strategy raise job performance? In organization, work performing is affected by job characteristics and physical work environment, ability and skills and the willingness to performance to the individual employee. The major strategic rewards decisions to reward employees which include: What to pay employees, how to pay individual employees, cognition programs? Concerning about what to pay? The employer needs to establish a pay structure balance between internal equity, (the value of the job for the organization) and external equity , the external competitiveness of an organization's pay relative to pay in its industry.

What does reward management mean? The management discipline is concerned with the formulation and implementation of strategies and policies, the purpose of which are to reward employees fairly, equitably and consistently in accordance with their value to the organization. It deals with design, implementation and maintenance reward systems (processes, practices, procedures) that aim to meet the needs of both the organization and its stakeholder. Thus, total reward can include non-financial as well as financial element is developed, implemented and treated. Usually , the components of total reward include two aspects: tangible rewards (base pay, contingent pay and employee benefits) as well as relational intangible rewards (learning and development), the work experience and achievement, growth , non-financial rewards . Then, it is the total reward. However, reward can include these tangible and intangible elements: payment, such as salary, bonus, shares etc. Praise, such as positive feedback, commendation, staff-of -the year award etc. Promotion, such as status, career development. Punishment, such as disciplinary action, criticism, withholding pay. Thus, if one employee can not achieve the satisfactory performance, he/she ought need to get disciplinary action to be punished in order to let he/she learns how to revise his/her performance to raise working efficiency.

How to implement strategic reward management? Where do we want our reward practices to be in a few years time (vision)? How do we intend to get these (mean)? So, a declaration of intent that defines what the organization wants to do in the longer term to develop and implement reward policies, practices and processes, that will further the achievement of its business goals, and need the needs of the stakeholders, it can give a framework to other elements of rewards. So, the structure and content of a reward strategy may include: Environment analysis, macro-level, social, economical, demographic, industrial level, and micro-level competitors, analysis of job evaluation, financial conditions, gap analysis.

When the organization expected to apply reward strategy to raise employee individual performance successfully? It needs to know what job evaluation means. It is a systematic process for defining the relative worth/size of the jobs roles within a organization, for establishing internal relatives, for designing an equitable grade structure and grading jobs in the reward structure. For example, reward strategy can attempt to reduce wage gaps, when the wage gap can occur in the company, it can use international benchmarking in job evaluation. However, the cause is simple. The market of top managers is usually international, they earn international wage, or they leave the firm. The market of workers with little or no qualification is local in nearly every case. They can earn local wages. In less developed countries , this can lead to raise wage gaps between the top and bottom employee. Hence, if the firm discovered it has large distance of wage gaps between its top and bottom level positions. It ought need to find methods to adjust these positions' salaries to be reduce large distance of wage gaps fairly in order to let these large distance of wage gaps of position employees , they can feel their company is more fair to treat every employee.

Moreover, firm also need to consider that whether it ought choose which type of individual payment to excite its employee individual performance to be improved. They may include: performance -related increases basic pay or bonus -related to assessment of performance, contribution-related pay is related both to inputs and outputs, skilled-base pay is related to high or low skilled to the individual effort performance, service -related pay is related to whether the employee needs to spend how long service-time to satisfy customer's need in order to measure every service employee's performance, team-based pay is related to team performance, it can encourage teamwork, loyalty and cooperation and it can be demotivating on individual level.

All of these any types of reward method will improve or encourage the low performance employee individual working efficiency or raise productivity more easily as well as fair reward strategy can upgrade the high performance employee individual efficiency or encourage them to exceed their productive level or raise their productivity to achieve the maximum number. Hence, reward management has direct relatively to influence every employee's performance in order to bring either long term positive or negative influence to their organizations.

1.3 What factors can influence organization's reward strategy?

What is reward management strategic principle to employment relationship? employees needs to pay tangibles (salary, wage, cars, educational , holiday allowance etc.) or/and intangible (recognition, career development growth etc.) rewards to employees aim. Individual balance to achieve tangible output, sales and/or intangibles loyalty , service performance, commitment. Hence, reward management forms the employment relationship, if an HR manager is to succeed in successfully managing the employment relationship, he/she will have to do well in reward management.

The reward management principle includes simplicity, it must be easily understood by everyone in the organization, fairness and equitability , every component of the system must be justifiable applied. This element is arguably the most challenging to implement and is the cause of most reward management related problems , such as strike, turnover, dissatisfaction etc. Hence, an attractive communication and training to the low skillful labour to have chance to upgrade high skillful which is needed, a participatory chance is effective one should ideally be negotiated and agreed between management and employees.

In fact, traditionally companies have always adopted the base pay strategy. It pays the legal minimum wages and salaries. However, it does not adequate in new work cultures and in terms of attracting , retaining and motivating top performers for strategic purposes, but still very commonly for lower level employees. The new reward strategic options include as below:

1. Knowledge and skills based strategy, because of the proven relation job performance, organizations have sought to encourage continuous skills development by trying it to rewards. A organization simply varies its pay structure according to one's level of knowledge and skill (job evaluation systems. It can define which skills, it values and will pay for and must have a supportive training and development strategy. It is based pay with an equal base pay and a variation based on skills and knowledge. It may be costly in the short-term , but it is beneficial from a knowledge HR base through increased productivity and quality of product.

2. Performance based (varied pay based structure strategy), employees should be rewarded only for the value they

create. A company will reward employee in the same grade variably depending on each employee's performance.
3. Incentive based pay structure strategy, it measures but being different in that it focuses on group performance rather than individual performance. The starting point in strategy is to define group performance targets , such as productivity sale volumes or profitability.
What factors can influence organization's reward strategy? They include: Affordability, the argument is that an organization can't borrow to reward employees, but it should reward from the value created by the employees themselves; legislation sets the minimum base pay minimum fixed pay rate; union/workers committees' pay level are determined through collecting bargaining. For example, strike issue will bring higher salary level in possible; external job value, the market value of the job, e.g. what is the market value of an HR manager or clerical assistant; internal job value, perceived value of job compared to the other jobs which the organization will determine the reward for the jobs , e.g. HR manage compared to finance manager; value of the person, employees holding similar jobs can be paid differently depending on the value to the organization performance; the economy changing factor (labor supply/ demand) in labor market, e.g. it is a depressed economy increases the supply of labour, it will reduce the labour wage/salary market prices, due to the economy is bad , employers won't need to raise to any employees number and it has excess labour supply number to affect reward policy strategy.

1.4 What is reward system of McDonald ?

For McDonald's Corporation U.S. employees at corporate, division and region offices, McDonald benefits are organized into four Performance management includes processes that effectively communicate , company aligned goals, evaluate employee performance and reward them fairly.
Your Pay and Rewards (ref from McDonald's reward system)
Attractive program follows a "pay for appearance" beliefs: The better your results, the greater your pay opportunities.

- Base Pay

Since employees' bottom pay is the most important portion of their recompense, McDonald's maintain the competitiveness of our base pay through an annual review of both external market data and interior peer data. In our business, division and region offices, McDonald's has a broad banding compensation system. Broad banding allows for suppleness in terms of pay, movement and growth.

- Incentive Pay

Inducement pay gives our workers with the possibility to earn spirited total compensation when performance meets and exceed goals. For our corporate, parting and region office, the Target Incentive Plan (TIP) links employee presentation with the presentation of the business they hold up. TIP pays a gratuity on top of employees' base salaries base on business presentation and their person appearance.

- Long Term Incentives

Long term incentives are granted to entitled workers to both prize and retain key employees who have shown continued presentation and can crash long-term value creation at McDonald's. for the befits of employees the long term incentives are very helpful because when the organization has a policies of incentives or long term incentives then the employees of the organization feel secured and work hardly for the organization. Similar like this any company or any Originations rewarding system always brought positive crash.

● Recognition Programs

Mc Donald's recognition programs are intended to reward and recognize physically powerful performers. For our corporate, separation and region offices, these take in the president Award (given to the top 1% of individual performers worldwide) and the Circle of fineness Award (given to top teams worldwide to be familiar with their aid for advancing our vision). Once start to hesitation your honesty, and then no one is leaving to alter their activities Appraisal system is also very helpful and makes a positive competition and encouragement in between the employees of the organization. Promotions will be appraisal based which encourage employees for hard work.

● Company Car Program

Mc Donald's company car program provides entitled employees with a company car for both business and individual / personal use. If entitled, employees can decide from. This is also very encouraging and motivating incentive for employees. It creates competition between employees and they work hard to get this incentive.

In conclusion, the assumptions the company is creation about their prospect service and its intention to support their progress. Practical processes for deploy people and delivering enlargement which are consistent with these intention. The reserve and promise for taking these types of program used. If we see in past we can get that simple ways in which the company could use the out test for the planed strategies and special and important clues for the good results.

Reference

Craig, E.A. & Stephen, L.M. & John, L.W. (2011) family business compensation: New Ycrk, US, Palgrave Macmillan, p.35

Leon, M. (2002). High performers, how the best companies find and keep them: US, Jossey - Bass, John Wiley & Sons, Inc, US pp.133-134

Robert P. V, (6 edition, 2006). organizational behavior: core concepts: US, Thomson, pp.58

CHAPTER TWO

ORGANIZATIONAL DEVELOPMENT

Why do organizations need develop?

Organizational development (OD) is defined by theorists and practitioners in different ways. Essentially, it is a planned, organization-wide effort to increase an organization's effectiveness and/or to enable an organization to achieve its strategic goals. Before working on organizational development activities, an essential first step is to map the organizational context in which the changes , you are hoping what will occur. It means to understand function what affect your work, which approach you may be bringing to the activities and being able to determine an organization's readiness to work with you and develop for themselves the required innovations.

Many OD projects focus on providing the more visible material resources, building skills, improving organizational structures and systems. Moreover, culture values have an impact on several elements of as including: the way change occurs, perception about whether change is needed, perception about leadership and ownership , perception about risk and uncertainty, perception about relationship and partnership and perception of what success looks like. It is described internal changes as relating to organizational structures, processes and human resource requirement, whereas external changes involves government legislation, competitor movements and customer demand.

In general, organizational development aims to expect to raise awareness, e.g. improved understanding, attitude, confidence or motivation , enhanced knowledge and skills, e.g. increasing ability to act through teamwork, e.g. strengthened ability to act through improved with a group a people tied by a common task. This may involve for example, among them members, a stronger agreement or improved, communication, coordination, contribution by the team members to the common task, enhanced networks, e.g. improved processes for stronger incentives for participation in the network or increased traffic or communication among network members; increased implementation know -how , e.g. discovery and innovation with learning by doing formulation or implementation of policies, strategies, plans for UD aims in possible.

Why do organizations need to changed? Our business would is fasting to increase technology new methods of production and new taste of customers and new market trends as well as new strategies for best control of the organizations and motivation of employees like to accept to use new products in popular nowadays. Hence, managers need to concern how to decide about the change management in the organizations, because business activities now are globalize, and every organization needs to attract loyal customers , trained the employees, introduce and adapt new methods of production and best control the activities of the organization.

How will change organization in the good condition? The question arises in present scenario. Organizational change or change management aims to raise ability of the management benefits and support from change with reduced inefficiencies and ineffectiveness from the side of employees and encourage appreciate acceptance and support. The process of changing the activities of the organization as well as the implementation of the procedures and technologies to achieve the design objective. If the organization usually needs to change management includes different aspects, such as control change, adaptation change and effecting change.

Consequently, organizational change simply means to change the activities of the organization, it concerns change the culture of the organization, technology, business process, change of employees, rules and procedures, recruitment and selection, design of jobs, methods of appraisal , human resource , technology, physical environment of the organization, methods of training and development, job skill, and knowledge etc.

However, when the organization decides to implement change. Some employees should feel not adapt the change easily. They will quickly respond by complaints, engaging in work slowdown, threating to go on strike etc. How to overcome change management implementation successfully. The organizations need to implement change fairly , selection people who accept change, education and communication.

However, organization development also plays an important role in the change management. It can be defined as a collection planned change, built a humanistic values and benefits and welfare needs, that need to improve the organizational effectiveness and employees work performance and well-being.

- Why does General Motor organization need change management?

For General Motor (GM) change management case example, GM taking swift cost cutting action (2008) showed GM established in 1908s, till 1920s it was becoming the world largest motor manufacturing company, it could produce new style and design car every year. These were different brand cars which were producing by the company that time, and this every there were no other competitors to compete in the company different cars. But, the Japan automakers the company, GM felt threatened, specially Toyota Japan. Hence, GM needed to again get his position in market by restructuring and making change in the company. Now the GM company is again operating business in core brands in America, such as GMC.

GM taking swift cost cutting action (2008) also indicated that however, the change to GM was the high wages cost to employees as the company was paying US$74 per hour as compared to Toyota US$44 per hour, because GM was an agreement with trade union and GM run the plant with minimum 80% capacity whether it was needed or not.

Hence, what types of changes are decided to bring or make change to GM. In fact GM decided to bring changes on some areas of the motor business. These were included, structural change, cost change, process change and cultural change. The steps which as taken to change by the GM is about cost cutting, it has reduced cost of some brands to maintain the profit level. Similarly , GM also cut pay of employees which was the major problem. The GM also changed the culture of the company. GM removed it automate producing board and automate strategy up to 8 men board. It can changed the culture to improve the efficiency of the employees and such change is to speed up the day to day decision making.

But, GM also encounters problems to change process. Such as problems in cultural change, the cultural plan was based top down approach, which ignored totally the involvement of the employees as compared to other companies, some suggested that it has not down up approach in which employees feel satisfaction. So this regard , it empowered the employees by introducing in tailoring the down top approach. Rather then telling to employees what they do, due to its employees hope have change to discuss with top management to express their opinions. Moreover, the other problem with cost cutting from the agreement of trade union, as it was an agreement with not lowering the pay of the employees and maintain the capacity level.

Driving change at GM (2005) indicated that better result of cost cutting of GM seems from its employment figure of 98 to 2009. It was reduced from 226,000 to 101,000 workers and now the GM is concentrating on sale rather than to further cut off and also GM is deciding to reduce the worker force of the factory from 60,000 to 40,000. It certainly leads to cost saving to GM. Another better result of cultural change to GM, employees now becoming aware about the responsibility, as well as GM as empowered the employed to give better productivity. Hence, GM can success to solve change management problems to bring profit and win its competitors in motor sale market in global successfully.

- Culture can influence organization development

Culture is not the way we do things around here. Culture is which we cooperate and the through we view the organization. If we view an organization as a system of interacting and interrelated part, culture defines , creates and supports that system.

- IBM computer organizational culture influences whether it's computers will be out dated feeling to computer consumers

For IBM computer example, IBM had brought to change a culture means changing our fundamental view of how the world works. However, IBM ran into serious financial difficulties in the late 1980 and early 1990s in large part because it was unwilling to change the ways in which it was approaching the computer market, even though the market was rapidly changing around it to break with tradition.

How is culture created to IBM? Stephen, R.B(2011) indicated IBM founder , or the influential leader, had reinforced the values of culture. When he worked for IBM many years ago, he discovered the IBM leader was one considerable person to his employees. Such as one case, how when an IBM employee was badly injured and his family killed in a car accident, the leader Tom Watson was there at the hospital when the man woke up, promising to cover the medical bills and do whatever he could. Hence, he can let IBM employees feel that IBM was seem to their home family.

Hence, what makes a successful culture to IBM ? Stephen, R.B(2011) also showed that a culture is successful if it is in harmony with its environment and unsuccessful if it it unable to function in its environment. The environment is the world in which the culture operates. So, when environment changes faster than cultures. When the environment changes, the mechanisms of the culture may no longer be valid. Such as the advent of the PC changed the business environment for IBM, and the company found it difficult indeed to adjust. Today, with the accelerating shift from desktop computers to mobile devices and the Internet, Microsoft is still. In 1992, IBM had a loss for the first time, closed down numerous divisions. However, IBM's culture contained a very strong ethic of " analyze the problem, determine the solution, and execute the solution even, if it 's unpleasant." IBM realized that it needed a fresh perspective, so it brought in Lou Gerstner, the first non-IBM to become CEO. As Ed Schein points out, Gerstner came from a very similar marketing background to IBM's founder, Tom Watson, Sr. Gerstner didn't so much change IBM's culture as revitalize an aspect of it that had become dormant. Over the year, IBM's engineering culture had become dominant, and the marketing culture had benefit to become into the background.

- IKEA organizational culture influences whether it's China furniture market in success?

Why does IKEA management cultural diversity needs to regard its staffs in China challenge? Multinational company, such as IKEA furniture company aims to increase profitability and it also needs to seek to for solutions to problems related with the saturation of existing markets, it needs to make an effort to expand operations to overseas market, such as China. However, it will face cultural difference challenge to be needed to deal if it want to enter China furniture sale market successfully.

Kumar, S. (2005) indicated IKEA is the world's largest furniture retailer since the early 1990s. It offers a wide range of well- designed, functional home furniture products at low prices as many people as possible will be able to afford them. However, IKEA planned to enter China market, but it will face the cultural difference challenge between China and itself Swedish regional cultural of their staff communication and co-operational relationship.

In deed, the "IKEA" facilities its successfully international expansions , it needs to combination vision, characteristic leadership and business principle between China and Swedish culture effectively. IKEA opened its first store in China in 1998. Although, the company has succeeded with their global strategy in the past in most of the markets, it has entered , it quickly learnt the success in the Chinese market required a different strategy in the areas of marketing and HR (Kumar, 2005, p.2).

What are the cultural difference to influence IKEA's success to develop furniture sale in China market? The standardized strategy which is adopted by IKEA could lead to some disadvantages because Swedish managers are needed to send to other branches in other countries in other to ensure the IKEA way is implemented in the local areas. Thus, it brings the conflict between the Swedish management and local employees could occur due to the cultural differences. Especially, in the country like China where the traditional cultures and value are different to such as Swedish culture. So, Chinese employees will have their mind for long a working culture differs from the Swedish way that IKEA wants to influence to their employees, problems were unavailable.

When IKEA were keen to increase revenue in Asian markets like China, they faced the challenge to mange their staffs from the conflicts and the diversity of Chinese cultures, such as how to train people within IKEA perform in a standardized format to keep its essential value, and how to avoid the misunderstanding when improve employee performance and understanding the importance of cross cultural management between Sweden and China. So, IKEA managers definitely have responsibilities to spend time, energy and effort to understand the differences of national corporate and functional cultures before starting an arranging the strategic plans in China furniture sale market.

The another cultural difference challenge concerns China and Sweden both countries have problems on law, price competition, information, language, delivery, foreign currency, time differences and cultural differences etc. different aspects. Thus, such as this IKEA Sweden furniture international company plans to enter China furniture sale market. It will have great barriers are caused by cultural differences, such as difficulty of communication, higher potential transaction costs, different objectives and means of cooperation and operating methods.

These problems have led to the failure to IKEA furniture to enter China furniture sale market in possible. Therefore, IKEA needs to concern questions how to do business in China and understand China's culture and how to do business with Chinese people. It is possible that Chinese labors dissatisfy IKEA's provided cheap labor as well as the strong serious organizational bureaucracy system, high job duty demand is needed to satisfy customer's behavior in China. Hence, IKEA's culture difference challenge to China furniture sale market , it has relationship to human resource management and reward challenge.

● HR development aims

Human Resource Development is the framework for helping employees develops their personal and organizational skills, knowledge, and abilities. Organizations have many opportunities for human resources or employee development, both within and outside of the workplace. By the end of this paper i will be able to devise a human resource plan for a work area, to meet organizational objectives, identify and plan for individual development to meet organizational objectives and also initiate a personal development plan for an individual and evaluate progress. Healthy organizations believe in Human Resource Development and cover all of these bases.

The focus of all aspects of Human Resource Development is on developing the most superior workforce so that the organization and individual employees can accomplish their work goals in service to customers. We need to learn new skills and develop new abilities, to respond to these changes in our lives, our careers, and our organizations. We can deal with these constructively, using change for our competitive advantage and as opportunities for personal and organizational growth, or we can be overwhelmed by them. With all the downsizing, outsourcing and team building, responsibility and accountability are being downloaded to individuals. So everyone is now a manager. Everyone will need to acquire and/or increase their skills, knowledge and abilities to perform their jobs. By developing our knowledge and skills, our actions and standards, our motivation, incentives, attitudes and work environment we will be able to cope up with the ever changing work environment.

Reference

Driving change at general motor, 2005, online retrieved 15 Dec. 2009,
www.cioleadershipnotes.com/p/gm/htm

General motor talking swift cost cutting action, 2008, online retrieved 15 Dec. 2009 from dailymarkets.com/stock/2008/11/24/General- motor- takingswift-cost-action-cutting

Kumar, S. (2005) "IKEA's globalization strategies and its foray in China", IBS center for management research

Stephen, R.B. Organizational development, U.S., The McGraw- Hill , 2011, pp.5-8

CHAPTER THREE

HUMAN RESOURCE ROLE IN BUSINESS

HR function in organization

HR role in business functions: HR ethics and code of industry includes that HR people should act legally, ethically and professionally as these aspects: Act legally, it represent the most core of obligations. HR is responsible for keeping current with changes in employment law and keeping management informed of risk or possible library. Act ethically, HR represents all employees at all levels of the organization, regardless of sex, age , race , color, material status, religion, disability or other protected class. At the same time, HR promotes the ethical culture of an organization. They must model the highest level of ethical behavior, administer all company policies and procedures fairly in handling disciplinary.

HR must conduct thorough investigations and make recommendations or decisions based on facts. Act professionally, HR must keep employees‘ and companies’ information in the strictest confidence and protect company information when dealing with employees or individuals outside of company. HR must follow changes in employment law, company policies and employment issues. They are also responsible for continuing education to remain expects in the field to be a successful strategic business partner. HR staffs need own business knowledge and understand the cost of people-related activities and responsible for measurement to all HR programs and processes, subject matter expert, in this role, the HR person should passes HR knowledge in relation to the most up-to-date employment law at the best HR practices for sourcing and staffing, remuneration strategy and systems, performance management, employee relations, and people development and advice business as appropriate.

At all time, a professional HR will keep his/her management informed of any potential risk and liability to the business , due to the change of employment law. Creating good working environment, HR needs to motivate , engage, contribute good and happy working environment to le staffs to work in the organization. HR needs to help to establish and promote the organizational culture in which people are willing to do the best performance to the jobs, and commit customer’s needs and concerns.

In this role, the HR person identifies and facilitates overall talent management strategies, employee development opportunities, employee assistance programs, long term incentive and effective communication opportunities and channels between management and employees. HR is such as one change agent. The HR person needs to know how to link changes to the strategic needs of the organization and being able to show empathy and concern employee needs to minimize employee dissatisfaction change. So, HR person needs have the ability to execute successful change strategies.

HR functions in organization include: workforce planning, sourcing staffing, organizational development, skills training , learning , talent development, reward management, compensation and benefits, employee relations, communication, engagement, HR policy and legal recommendation, change management, employee welfare, workplace health and safety.

Staffing sourcing means the success plan or buy recruit from external. It is a process , a company ensures that employees are recruited and developed to fill the key roles. Through high-performing employees, develop their knowledge, skills and capability and prepare them for advancement or promotion into even more challenging roles in 3 to 5 years' time. So, it asks to develop the employees to special projects, team leadership roles, internal and external movement to training and development opportunities.

The success plan should identify key position, its key roles and contributions, key success factors of key positions, skill, knowledge, capabilities, reasons cause of turnover, potential success identification, development plans for potential successor to reach the required success factors.

Recruit from external or buying recruiting resource from the labour market is suitable to meet company short-term staffing needs for the junior to middle level positions. It can help new skills and new experience. Sources of supply can be from a combination of full time/part time employees, recruitment agencies' temporary workers and contract workers.

The contracting applicants arrangement stage means the HR needs to contract the job applicants and invite for an interview, conducts the job interview, prepares the resume in advance and highlight areas to require further during the interview, knowledgeable about the company, the role in discussion and the job application process the applicants able to answer questions they might have, enthusiastic , friendly and courteous , so the applicant will be viewed the opportunity move positively, resourceful and helpful to hire managers , such as sharing tips ar interviewer, how to manage interviewees' expectation etc.

Arranging interview stage providing the shortlisted candidates with helpful information about the interview includes: when and where the interview, who will be in the interview, how the interview will be conducted. Facilitating effective interview, the interviewer needs to ensure the interviewing environment is comfortable one free no noise, not leave the candidate waiting for too long. When closing the interview, the interviewer should advise the candidate of the possible must steps, online screening of application forms, using online to search and compare job applicant's information, job skills, years of experience, education level to identify suitable candidates for further selection processes.

Reward management is concerned with the formulation and implementation of strategies and policies that aim to reward people fairly, equitably a fact, employers nowadays can hardly rely solely on base salary to attract and motivate their employees. More emphasis has other benefits , such as retirement benefits and learning opportunities. Performance and reward system should be market-based, equitable and cost-effective. Rewards do not only depend on skills, capabilities and experience of individuals, but also performance. In order to encourage top rate performers, employers must not only offer rewards for good work, but they must also have consequences for substandard work. Although, employers usually do not want to follow through with negative consequences, it is sometimes a necessary process. Otherwise, employees have no incentive to correct unacceptable behavior.

Employers also needs to clearly know about what is recognized by the company and how these will be measured. So that they understand the relationship of performance and reward. Total reward may include anything value resulting of employment relationship to the employee with a goal to attract, motivate and attract talent. It can include financial and non-financial rewards and that these can change over time depending on their personal circumstances. Employers need to find out what attracts, engages individuals and explore how best they can meet these needs. It is important that the company how design's the elements of the reward package to support.

What factors can determine rewarding for performance, qualification, experience, potential, behavior, effort, achieving goals, meeting targets. How the employees will be rewarded, the awards whether are company's work culture/characteristics are whether driven the right behavior/performance/efforts the awards are be valued by the employees, the awards are how often to be given, how often the rewards are reviewed, the award is long or short term.

Legal framework for reward system , such as payment of wage, restriction on wages deduction, minimum wage, benefit, such as share options or housing benefits. Major benefit plans may include: retirement benefit schemes, personal security, e.g. healthcare, dental , hospitalization, accident or life insurance, financial assistance, e.g. mortgage interest subsidies, rental subsidies, staff discount, education subsidies, personal needs, e.g. holidays and leave with pay child care, fitness and facilities, use of holiday house, employee shares purchase plan, company car etc. welfares.

3.1 What is HR's role in corporate social responsibility?

The HR function should help formulate and achieve environmental and social goals when also balancing these objectives with traditional financial performance metrics. The HR function can serve as a partner in determining what is needed or what is possible in formulating corporate values.

At the same time, HR should play a key role in ensuring that employees implement the strategy consistently. For example, encouraging employees, through training and compensation to find ways to reduce the use of environmentally damaging chemicals in the products, assisting employees in identifying ways to recycle products that can be used for play grounds for children who do not have access to healthy places to play designing a company's HRM system to reflect equity development avoid well-being , thus contributing to the long-tem health.

How HR policies shape the workplace and how HR can improve employee well-being through better working conditions and more positive workplace a cultures. Top-management can encourage particularly supervisory support, also has been identified as key to employee environment actions. In addition, adopting HRM and communicating a pro-environmental image can have a positive reputational effect. This helps to staff , the company leading to lower recruitment and training costs and a better financial bottom line. In fact, in some cases, a pro-environmental stance may be more important to potential employees. It can help a company address wider social problems that are affecting not only its external community, but also the company's financial bottom line. For example, The US postal service employees participate in more than 80 cross-functional teams across the US do drive energy reduction and resource conservation. These teams helped the postal service reduce energy, water, solid waste to landfills and petroleum fuel use as well as recycles more than 222000 tons of material. Thus, HR-related activities that can support , such as responsible workplaces, human rights, safety practices, labor standards, performance developments, diversity, employee compensation and more.

● Human resource role in Hong Kong business environment

Andy, W.C. el.(2002) indicated that economic
downturn which began in early 1998 had dramatic effects on Hong Kong's prosperity and increasing rates of Gross Domestic Product, especially during the 1990s and the early years of the 21st century. In late 2002s, Hong Kong's unemployment rate stood at 7 per cent and showed no immediate prospect of diminishing. This has huge implication for human resource professionals and especially for their training, as managers of the organization's most precious resource, its people. Moreover, downsizing and consequent increases in the rate of unemployment were logical consequences of this process.

However, Hong Kong's strengths in finance, trade, services and tourism provided benefits from the effects of these recessionary forces. But, Hong Kong was faced with the poor of dealing with the human resource implications and other aspect of workforce reduction. Hence, it explains why HK organizations need to consider HRM functions as part of the acquisition, development , motivation and maintenance of human resources in order to bring direct relevance of the strategic decision-making on which profits and productivity depend.

Human resource management is focused on the development and application of policies in relation to human resource planning, recruitment, selection, placement, and termination, management education , training and career development, terms of employment and methods and standards of remuneration, working conditions and employee services, formal and informal communication and consultation through employer and employee representative at all levels, negotiation and implementation of agreements on wages and working conditions , as well as procedures for the avoidance and settlement of disputes and the creation of a fairer and more equitable workforce in which discrimination in any form is viewed as unethical behaviors.

HRM responsibilities include to conduct research into local wage levels to ensure the firm's reward system is competitive with those in other companies, devising remuneration systems to excite or encourage or persuade workers into enhanced effort and efficiency, administering superannuation schemes, e.g. retirement welfare plan, and advising employees about their pensions, maintaining personnel records and statistics, preparing accurate job descriptions and other retirement documentation, implementing health and safety regulations, accident prevention and the provision of first-aid facilities, e.g. safe construction site environment, designing and evaluating management training and development schemes linked with succession planning and developing and implementation systems with facilities organizational communication.

Role of HR manager includes the control function, such as analysis of key operational data in human resource areas of labor turnover, wage cost, absenteeism, monitoring of staff performance (staff appraisal) and recommending appropriate remedial action to managers; the advisory function offers expect advice on human resource policies and procedures, e.g. which employees are ready for promotion, who should attend a certain training course, arrangement contracts of employment, health and safety regulations etc. related human resource related issues.

The future role of HR manager needs to concern to adopt an international insight in their work, growing concern for the application of ethical approaches to human resource management, implementation of equal opportunity , data privacy, and arranging flexible working models, such as job sharing, job rotation, permanent part –time work, increased awareness to encourage or persuade for effective employee participation in company production systems in order to achieve raising efficiencies and effectiveness, concerning the consequences for HR management of the ageing workforce discussed issues, such as prolonging / shortening working age or shortening /prolonging retirement age policy, participating legal system in human resource issues, including laws on hiring , dismissing, equal opportunities, age, country discrimination conduct of industrial relations.

HR planning can help management in making decision in the following areas: recruitment. , avoidance of redundancies (increasing labor turnover, training, management and development, estimates of labor cost, productivity bargaining, raising effectiveness or efficiency , accommodation requirements. In order to achieve company's maximum benefits purpose, HR planning needs continuous readjustment (annual review) , because the goals of an organization are subject to change and its internal and external environment is uncertain. It is also complex because it involves to many independent variables, e.g. increasing skillful immigration job seeker number to compete in the country's local labor market or decreasing skillful labor, e.g. computer programmers, doctors, accountant, lawyers etc. occupation professionals sudden emigrate to other countries to seek jobs, consumer demand increases or decreases to the product. Hence , it must include feedback because if the plan can not be achieved, the objectives of the company will have to be modified so that they are feasible in human resource terms.

The human resource plan process to one company is a cycle process. The first step may include that it needs to follow issues from corporate plan's strategies and objectives. The main points to be considered such as capital equipment plans, reorganization, e.g. centralization or decentralization, how to change in product or in output, marketing plans and financial limitations.

After it gathers the company's corporate strategic plan data. Then, it will implement its second step. This step may include three aspects:

- How to achieve the reasonable present utilization of human resources in particular: numbers of employees in various categories, estimation of labor turnover for each grade of employee and the analysis of labor effects of high or low turnover rates on the organization's performance, amount of overtime worked, amount of short time, appraisal of performance and the potential of present employees and general level of payment compared with that in other comparable firms. All these HR related data is essential to be recorded in accurate attitude.
- The external environment of the company analysis, such as recruitment position, population trends, local housing and transportation plans, government policies in education and retirement.
- The potential supply of labor analysis, such as effects of local emigration and immigration, effects of recruitment or redundancy in local firms, possibility of employing categories not now employed, for example outsource employees number, part time and semi-retired workers number and changes in productivity , working hours.

The final step is that HR planning needs to be achieved. It includes recruitment/redundancy program, training and development program, industrial relations policy and accommodation plan. The issues will appear in this plan, such as jobs which will appear, disappear or change, to what extent redeployment or retraining is possible, necessary changes at supervisory and management is possible, necessary changes and supervisory and management levels, training needs, arrangements for necessary and details of arrangements for handling any human problems arising from labor deficits or surpluses , e.g. early retirement or other natural wastage procedures. Following , it needs to give feedback , what will be possible modification to company objectives to company's corporate level to review its HR plan whether it can achieve company's objectives and strategic aims.

Human resource manager can be one human resource relation consultant to give recommendation how the organization should be better equipped to cope with the HR consequences of changed circumstances, careful consideration of likely future human resource requirements could lead the firm to discover new and improved ways surpluses might be avoided, it helps the firm to create and develop employee training and management succession program, some of the problems of managing change may be foreseen or consultations with affected groups and individuals can occur at an early stage in the change process and decision can be taken and by considering all the relevant , options, rather than being taken in crisis situations, management can assess critically the strengths and weaknesses of its labor force and HR policies, wasting or excess of effort among employees can be avoided and coordination to worker's efforts is improved to raise efficiencies and productive effectiveness.

- HR role in bank industry development

What is human resource (HR) role in organization? What factors can change to influence HR? They include workforce changes, globalization, ethics, organizational growth, increased accountability. These factors can influence HR's role change in the organization. So , when you assume be one HR manager, you need to concern : How have you used you awareness of internal and external changes to guide the decision making of your stakeholders ,e.g. discussing the impact of trends in workforce skills with function leaders? Which of your knowledge , skill, abilities or other characteristics have been useful in consulting with stakeholders?

Hence, HR role needs to understand the organizational goals and the role each function plays, serves of a cross-functional bridge. Locates talent throughout the global organization, identifies and supports need for resources or training, advices core functions on how with adapts to organizational strategy. Moreover, HR leaders need own knowledge of other business functions and whose organizations' business influences specific actions by HR , e.g. understanding the type of experts needed by R&D and future trends for that need. Also, the HR leader needs to know which of whose knowledge, skills, abilities or other characteristics have been useful in responding to this challenge?

HR also needs to consider how its organizational functions. They have disadvantages and advantages in order to achieve HR staff skill, talent to satisfy different departments' needs effectively and efficiently. Organizational structure has three types: Firstly, functional type advantages of easy to understand, specialization develop economies of scale, communication within function, career paths, fewer people and disadvantages of weak customer or product focus , potentially weak communication among function, hierarchical structure. Secondly, product type advantages of economies of scale, product team culture, product expertise and disadvantages of regional or local focus, more people, weak customer focus. Finally, geographic type advantages localization, quicker response time and disadvantages of fewer economic of scale, more people potential quality control.

HR also needs to concern when it's company needs to implement outsourcing employment need rea third party contractors' successful outsourcing depends on choosing the right activities to outsource, cooperation of contractor's performance objectives with strategic requirements.

Confirmation of contractors' reliability, capacity, expertise and ethical behavior. So , when the organization feel it needs to employ outsource contractors. The HR has responsibility to lead and know how to apply whose ethical practices competency in contracting for HR services or performing , due diligence or organizational sourcing, e.g. taking steps to protect employee data. The HR leader or manager also needs to know which of his/her knowledge skills, ability or other characteristics has been useful in responding to this challenge.

Standard chartered had have good talent management strategies to train its staffs. The talent management at standard chartered bank (SCB) features include: Standard chartered bank has good performance appraisal or measurement strategy. By making it a global standard to conduct face-to-face performance appraisals every six months. SCB is reviewing its own performance management objectives to make sure that those objectives stay relevant and achievable. Being sensitive to different cultures by employing different appraisal methods, also show that SCB understands the importance of managers and staff identifying and dealing with real, actual problems in a way that is most familiar and effective to them. Through appraisal, SCB also classifies their employees into 5 categories ranging from high potentials to critical resources, then to core contributors, followed by underachievers and finally underperformers. By identifying areas in which they are lacking and act.

What are the relevance HR problem to bring bank crisis to SCB. SCB view of employees as human capital in the organization, it could have at least minimized the less to a certain extent. For one, discussions between employers and still could have been more open and problem issues could have been identified at an earlier stage inefficiencies in the organization would have been uncovered , influence their performance against regional offices. In a way, having a certain amount of centralized control through talent management would also enable the monitoring of its offices globally.

What are performance appraisal aims? Performance appraisal is the measurement of the effectiveness of an employee's job performance. The process is described as the collection and use of judgements, ratings, perceptions or more objectives sources of information to understand better the performance of a person, team, unit, business, process program in order to guide subsequent actions and decisions. The result or performance outcomes represent the contributions that an individual's job performance makers to an organization and its goals.

Performance appraisal focus on measuring or appraising the job performance of a individual, e.g. use of surveys or rating focus to assess and evaluate employee behavior. It brings the either positive or negative feedback to the employee in the performance view and the new goals for the next performance period may be discussed.

3.4 HR role in India automobile industry

Human resource development (HRD) is the part of human resource management in any organizations. It deals with training employees in the organization when the industry feels it have need to upgrade skills to its staffs. It aims to let them to learn new skills distributing resources that are beneficial for the employee's task. For automobile industry in India example, India automobile sale companies will need effective HRD in their organizations if they expect to sell automobiles to global customers attractively.

Authors (May, June 2014) from internet essay indicated the India automobile sector is divided in four different sector which are as follow: two wheeler, which comprise of mopeds, scooters, motorcycles and electric two-wheelers passenger vehicles which include passenger cars, utility vehicles and multi-purpose vehicles, commercial vehicles that are light and material heavy vehicles and three wheelers that are passenger carriers and product carriers.

Why do India automobile sale companies need to concern HRD? Authors (May, June 2014) indicated the automobile industry is one of the key drivers that boost the economic growth to India. However, the year 2013-2014 has seen a decline in the industry's growth . High inflation , high interest rates, low consumer sentiment and rising fuel prices with economic slowdown and rising fuel reason for the downturn of the industry.

Except for the two wheelers, all other segments in the industry have been weakening. These is a negative impact on the automakers and dealers who offer high discounts in order to push sales. To match the decline in demand, automakers need good skillful of automakers to manufacturers attractive automobiles in order to attract foreign automobile buyers to choose to buy themselves any kinds of automobiles.

Despite the comprehensive market being under extreme burden, the luxury car market has observed a robust double digit like during the year 2013-2014, as a result of rewarding new launches at lower price points. Hence, foreign robust luxury cars competitors influence India automobiles sale number to be reduced. Hence, India automobile manufacturers felt automobile manufacturing workers' skills need to be train or improve in order to manufacture more comfortable and good design vehicles to satisfy future global automobile consumers' driving enjoyable needs.

In fact, India automobile industry employment opportunities will trend increase in the future with the number of vehicles available on the road today, the need and requirement for people who can fix these machines is fast increasing. The automobile jobs like automobile technician, car or bike mechanics are a great option. Becoming a diesel mechanic is also a significant alternative in India, auto labor market. Diesel mechanics are responsible for repairing and servicing diesel engines. As they are also required to repair engines of trucks and buses, other than cars. Even if communication with people instead of repairing cars in what interest to Indian, then Indian have opportunity of becoming a salesperson or sales manager in an automobile company. Career opportunities in automobile design, paint specialists, job on the assembly line and insurance of vehicles is also available.

Future India automobile industry employment trend is as the destination choice for design and manufacture of automobiles employers who need to automobile production skillful worker number will rise, because India manufacturing heavy vehicles, passenger vehicles, commercial vehicles automobile production skillful workers need number will rise.

Hence, India automobile sale employers will need have good human resource development model for the automobile companies, if they expect to raise automobile sale competitive effort in global automobile sale market. At the implementation level, India executives of the automobile companies need to strengthen their training, net working and more towards providing a satisfactory human resource development climate for its automobile industry car production, design, repair, salespeople employees and suggest suitable changes and corrections in the policy decisions for management of automobile companies and policy makers. Hence, future HRD practices in automobile industrial organizations for India automobile companies aim to identify the HRD mechanisms implemented in the selected automobile companies to achieve the training function to be effectively managed in the automobile companies in order to raise automobile sale competition effort in global automobile market.

3.5 Challenge of HR management

As a HR specialist, what are the challenges you may face and what HR intervention mechanisms would you consider using in an attempt to drive individual and organizational performance in a multinational company? Critically evaluate this question by utilizing the appropriate academic literatures.

The challenges of the HR specialist when there engage in attempt of increasing the individual and organizational performances in Multinational Companies through developing a set of HRM best practices, especially relating to employee recruitment and selection, performance management and staff retention. Since the organizations are multinational number of concerns are arises such as dealing cultural issues with the organizational goals as well as individual goals. Furthermore organizational behaviors and tools such as engagement, motivation and empowerment are basically highlighted; without those it is merely a dream to achieving the business goals. Basically Multinational companies are aiming profits and there for individual and organisational performance are very vital for their existence.

HR has been organized in a different ways over the years. Some functions have emphasized delivery by location or by business structure. In these models an integrated HR team has serviced managers and employees at specific location or with in specific businesses units, with some more strategic or complex tasks reserved for the corporate center. The degree to which these different arms of HR were centralized or co-located and the question of whether they were managed by the business unit varied. Within the HR teams, depending up on their size their might have been specialization by work area (especially for industrial relations in the 1960s and 1970s) or by employee grade or group (responsibility, say, divided between those looking after clerical staff from those covering production) The advancement of personal management starts around end of the 19th century, when welfare officers came in to being.

There are some organizations where HR is seen as a central, corporate function with little advancement to business units. Some other organizations position themselves in the opposite direction, with a very small corporate center and all the activity distributed to business units. The question of best structure is how the function best organizes itself between the pulls of centralization and the pushes of decentralization.(The changing HR functions) The HR assumptions and HR practices observed in high performing firms are the key elements to the formation of the Best Practice theory. Employment security, selective hiring, self managed teams, high pay contingent on company performance, extensive training, reduction of status difference, and sharing information are the key element of the theory. However less concern about the organisational goals and culture are given as draw backs for the theory. According to the “best fit theory” a firms that follows a cost leadership strategy designs narrow jobs and provides little job security, whereas a company pursuing a differentiation strategy emphasizes training and development. In other words this argues that all SHRM activities must be consistent with each other and linked to the strategic objectives of the business. HRM uses various technologies to direct employees behavior towards objectives and tasks that deliver approved organisational performance. Many organizations try to frame these ‘levers’ with an overall performance management system, and attach incentives and rewards to achievements of objectives and targets within this. HR will need to reduce employment expenses to help organizations to save income. Direct costs include: Recruitment costs (advertising, admin, etc.),Induction/training costs, other admin costs associated with new hires, Overtime/ cost of temporary workers, reduced productivity cost etc. which are related to HR expenses.

In conclusion there is evidence to suggest that including the practice out line within this organisational behaviours and tools can used to drive organisational and individual performance in Multinational companies. It is essential to have suitable recruitment and selection process, performance Appraisal System and staff Retention plan to ensure the right people, In the right place, at the right time with right attitude. Training and development is also vital to improve HR performance. In addition HR Specialists role will be more specific when these techniques applying in to multi cultural environments where people perceptions and behavioral patterns are different from each other.

3.6 The nature of the employment relationship

John, B. & Jeff, G. (6 edition, 2017) indicated Human resource management defines a distinctive approach to employment management, which seeks to achieve competitive advantage through the strategic deployment of a highly committed and capable workplace using an array of cultural, structural and personnel techniques. Also, human resource management is a strategic approach to managing employment relations which emphasizes that leveraging people's capabilities and commitment is critical to achieving sustainable competitive advantage or superior public services. This is accomplished through a distinctive set of integrated employment policies, program and practices in an organizational and societal context. Moreover, human resource management underscores the importance of people, only the " human factor" or labor can provide talent to generate value. It should draw attention to the notion of indetermination or uncertainty, which devices from the employment relationship: Employees have a potential capacity to provide the added value desired by the employer. It also follows from this that human knowledge and skills are a strategic resource that needs investment and skillful management. Moreover, in the environmental change factor influences to any organizations need to provide a role for HRM in improving an organization's performance in terms of overall sustainability.

● What is the nature of the employment relationship ?

The nature of the social relationship between employers and the social relationship between employees and employer is an issues of central analytical importance to HRM. The employment relationship describes a relation between employees (non-managers and managers) and their employer. Through the employment contract, inequalities of power structure both economic exchange (wage or salary) and the nature and quality of the work performed whether it is routine or creative. They can be short-term, primarily but not economic exchange for a relatively well-defined set of duties and low commitment or they can be complex long-term relationships defined by a range of economic inducements and relative security of employment, given in return for a set of duties and a high commitment from the employee.

Airline services: the demands of emotional labor of employment relationship between airline and airline staffs.

Positive emotion at work offers an apparent win to win situaton for airline organizations and individuals as it suggests that if a job or work is correctly designed, individuals will feel better and perform better. What was once a private act of emotion management is sold now as labor in the public contract jobs? What was once a privately negotiated rule of feeling or displaying is now set by th airline company's standard practices division. However, such as airline service waiter job, a private emotional system has been subordinated to commercial logic and it has been changed by whose airline employers.

● HR role in business maximizing efficiency method

John , H. (2013) described the work of police officers, we might discuss the functions of preventing come and catching criminals, the practices of patrolling, filling in report forms, breaking up disturbances, making arrests, and the qualities of commitment service. He also indicated police work is much more complicated than the brief suggestions and management work (including the management of police work) is much more complex still. It is hard to describe the functions without detailing the practices or to make sense of the practices without involving the functions.

John, H. (2013) defined characteristics of management is responsibility for an organization or organization unit and for the work of its members. The unit might be anything from a small retail outlet with one or two shop assistants to large corporation with tens or even hundreds of thousands of employees, but most managers are directly responsible for managing the organization of a manage number of people, typically between two and twenty and of the various processes in which they are engaged. So, we have sales managers and production managers and marketing managers and IT managers etc. organizing the work of specialists. The at the level, of the business unit or agency or regional subsidiary, we have general managers whose jobs is to organize and coordinate the work of different specialist groups.

Maximizing efficiency method

Maximizing efficiency was a work study or time-and-motion to be exercise designed to calculate how the work could be most efficiently carried out. This involved the analysis of different possible divisions of different possible tasks of labour into specialized tasks. The optimization of the tools and machines, and the optimization of the physical movements, required to operate them, assuming workers well suited to the specified tasks concern. The optimized system would then be so as to become a standard requirement to be implemented with absolute regularity, so that the whole workplace operated as a machine. Workers would be selected with the skills and strengths to perform each specialised task, and trained to follow the standard procedures. They would be fairly paid for what was scientifically established to be a reasonable level of performance (assuming they were well pay introduced, to encourage over-performance and punish (underperformance). Both owners or employee would benefits.

It indicated conclusion was that output was determined less by working conditions or incentive systems than by the informed social pattern of the work group. Feeling mattered and wherever managers took a personal interest in the workers, made them feel important and generated mutually supportive and cooperative environment, output are enhanced management. It seems was not about mechanical optimization processes, but about leadership and team dynamics. The management characteristics were however critical and with some rearrangement they can be summarized as follows: A strong people orientation, every body is treated s part of the team and just as an replaceable resource, flexibility and teamwork value driven value system is through the company.

- six situation factors can influence management's choice of HR strategy

Beer , M., et al. (1984) explained that HRM and the issue of management goals and specific HR outcomes. The Harvard framework consists of six basic components as below:

Beer, M., et al. (1984) indicated these six situation factors can influence management's choice of HR strategy. Firstly, situation factors include workforce characteristics, business strategy and conditions, management philosophy, labor market, unions , task technology , laws and societal values. Any one of situation factor can influence management's choice of HR strategy. The situation factor can bring influences to other two components. Stakeholder interests component means shareholders, management, employee groups, government, community, union as well as human resource management policy choices component, it means employee influence, human resource flow, reward system and works systems. It emphasizes that management' decisions and actions in HR management can be fully appreciated only if it is recognized that they result from an interaction between constraints and choices will be influenced by situational factor component and share holder interests components and long-term consequences component influences.

The human resource management policy choices component will influence the human resource outcomes component, it includes commitment, competence, cost -effectiveness. It means that it needs to understand the importance of management's goals, the HR outcomes of high employee commitment and competence are linked to longer term effects on organizational effectiveness and societal well-being.

The assumptions are built into the framework are that employees have talents that are rarely fully utilized in the workplace and that they show a desire to experience growth through work. The, the human resource outcomes component will influence the long-term consequences component. It includes individual well-being, organizational effectiveness and societal well-being . The long-term consequences distinguish between three goals: individual , organizational and societal. At the level of the individual employee, the long-term HR outputs comprise the psychological rewards that workers receive in exchange for their effort. At the organizational level, increased effectiveness ensures the survival of the firm. The societal level, as a result of fully utilizing people at work, some of society's goals (for example, employment and growth are attained.

Finally, the sixth component is a feedback loop component, it is through which the outputs flow directly into the organization and to the stakeholders. However, long-term outputs can influence situational factors, stakeholder interests and HR management policy choices in cycle two way relationship.

- Knowledge management at hotel industry

Hotels' realization led to the design and implementation of a computerized knowledge library that was accessible to every site manager in every hotel across the Australia/South pacific/ South East Asia region. The system was designed to initiate a long-term knowledge-sharing culture by making it easier to share value-added practices and processes, thus reducing wastage of time and resources through replication.

The problem- The knowledge library operated as a two way system whereby managers could both add ideas or effective innovative practices and find solutions to some of their own operational problems that demanded new ideas or innovation. To simplify its use, the system was designed to store ideas by hotel function (that is food and beverage, housekeeping etc.) with both functional and key word search tools available , knowledge transfer was considered to have occurred once an idea had been implemented at another site.

Hotel management realized that they would need to create support systems to motivate sharing between the sites and geographical regions. This opened up an opportunity to achieve the desired knowledge, sharing actions and behaviors. Throughout the performance management system, as a result, for each site manager to pass their annual performance review, they had to retrieve a minimum of two ideas from the system and implement these in their hotel, as well as add two ideas to the system for others to be able to access and use.

The idea that the hotel different site managers' knowledge and expertise can play a strategic role in achieving competitive goals to expect to achieve a strategy results in superior performance, or a competitive advantage. Achieving high performance, improving employment skills, pay-for -performance, profit sharing, performance appraisal, team working, job evaluation, information-sharing, employment security, selective hiring, self- managed teams or team working, high pay contingent on company performance, extensive training, reduction in status differences, information sharing(knowledge management) benefits.

- Manpower planning role in business

Manpower planning (workforce planning) means personnel and HR managers need to ensure that necessary supply of people was forthcoming to allow targets to be met. In theory at least, a manpower plan could show how the demand for people and their skills within an organization could be balanced by supply. The idea of a balance between demand and supply reflects the influence of the language of classical labor economics, in which movement towards an " equilibrium" serves as an ideal.

The utilization, improvement and preservation of an organization's human resources. The four stages of the planning process may include: the first stage is an evaluation or appreciation of the existing manpower resources. The second stage is an estimation of the proportion of currently employed manpower resources that were likely to be within the firm by the forecast data. the third stage is an essential or forecast of labor requirements needed if the organization's overall objectives were to be achieved by the forecast date and the fourth stage, it needs to measure to ensure that the necessary resources were available as and when required that is the manpower plan.

There were two main reasons for companies to use manpower planning. To develop their business objectives and manning levels and to reduce the " unknown" factor. Firstly organization implements strategy and targets, it brings organization practices and methods, it brings manpower review and analysis (internal and external factors) , it brings forecast (demand and supply), it brings adjust to balance (recruit, retain and reduce).

Way of working includes: annualized hours, working time organized on the basis of the number of hours to be worked over a year rather than a week; it is usually used to fit in with peaks. Compresses hours, which allows individuals to work their total number of agreed hours over a shorter period. Flexi-time, employees have a choice about their actual working hours, usually outside certain agreed core times. Home working, either on a fully time basis or an a part time basis where employees divide their time between home and office. Job-sharing , which involves two people employed on a part time basis but, working together to cover a full time post. Shift-working , giving employers the scope to have their business open for longer periods than an 8 hour day. Staggered hours, employees can start and finish their day at different times. Term-time working, employees can take unpaid leave of absence during the school holidays.

- Recruitment, selection and talent management stages include:

Internal factors and external factors bring to workforce planning staffing needs options: internal via external brings to recruitment attraction via sources brings to applicant pool brings to selection assessment brings to job performance measurement brings to job analysis brings to workforce planning staffing needs opinions in cycle processing again.

Capable people who will apply for jobs within a organization. First, there is a need to attract people's interest in applying for employment. It implies that people have a choice about which organizations they wish to work for, even though during times of recession such choices might be limited. People may be capable of fulfilling a role in employment, but the extent to which this will be realized is not totally predictable. How capability is understood is increasingly determined by an organization's approach to talent management and development.

Under different labour market conditions, power in recruitment process will change between buyers and sellers of labour, the employers and employees respectively. Thus, in conditions of recession, employers are likely to reduce recruitment budgets and costs, paying more attention to developing the talent that has already been employed.

● Online recruitment

Budgetary factors will also affect how recruitment channels are used, with more use of online recruitment. For example, the ageing profile of the workforce around the world requires an adjustment of recruitment policies, the use of the internet and agencies for recruitment reflected to younger applicants, whereas older workers were more dependent on formal channels of recruitment, such as newspapers and journals. In addition, there have been many more graduates leaving university, and graduate employment is becoming very competitive. Many graduates will take longer to find employment that matches their skills. This might affect perceptions of the value to be gained from studying for a degree compared with the price of a degree.

There is a difference, however, in what recruiters think is important to this generation and what the generation itself thinks . Although HR policies will be designed to achieve particular organizational targets and goals, those policies will also provide an opportunity for individual needs and be satisfied . This view assumes that a fit between a person and the environment can be found so that their commitment and performance will be enhanced.

This an indication that the person to environment fit includes a person to organization fit, person to group fit and person to environment fit. If there is a match between the values within each of those areas expressed by the organization at the recruitment stage. The organization and the new recruits have a clear employees and can therefore manage those expectations.

HRM could help to shape the direction of change, influence culture and help bring about the mindset that would decide which strategic issues more considered. HR considerations, including the results of a review of the quantity and quality of people, the goals , objectives and targets whether they can achieve performance in an organization and for how work is organized into roles and jobs.

There has been a rapid growth in online recruitment , e-recruitment. As a result, organizations are advised to consider the design of websites and the terms that applicants might use to carry out job and vacancy searches. The usability of a company's website affects an applicant's perception of a job, with a focus on hyperlinks and text rather than graphic images and navigation links. However, issues with e-recruitment , including the one-way communication system, the fact that it is impersonal and passive, and the fact that it creates an artificial distance between the individual and the company.

● recruitment agent

However, once a recruitment strategy has been formed, an organization might outcomes its implementation to reduce costs and take advantage recruitment expertise, especial a large number of staff are recruitment. Recruitment agents act as "labor market inter-mediaties" between individual recruits and recruiting organizations. Financial service organization assessment and measurement of creating customer service performance indicators include as below:

Anticipating customer needs and planning accordingly, identifying the customers who will be of value to the company, recommending change to current ways of working that will improve customer service, arranging the collection of customer satisfaction data and acting on them. The analysis and definition of competencies should allow the identification and isolation of behavior that are distinct and are associated with competent or effective performance. On this assumption, the assessment of competencies is one means selecting employees.

Recruitment channels may include walk in, employee referrals, advertising, particularly online job boards, websites, labour market intermediaries, such as social media , social professional networks, recruitment agencies, educational associations, professional associations.

- job description

Job description includes job title, department, reponsible to , relationships, purpose of job/overall objectives, specific duties and responsibilities, physical and economic conditions as well as personnel specification includes physical characteristics, general intelligence, specific attitudes, interests, impact on other people, qualification and experience, abilities, motivation. Both job description and personnel specifications have been key elements, it replies too much on the analyst's subjective judgement in identifying the key aspects of a job and the qualities that related to successful performance.

- Selection

An organization wishes to recruit new employees to define criteria against which it can measure and assess applicants. Increasingly , such criteria are set in the form of competencies composed of behavioral characteristics and attitudes. Organizations have become increasingly aware of making good selection decisions, as selection involves a number of costs include: the cost of the selection process itself, including the use of various selection instruments, the future cost of training new staff , the cost of labor turnover if the selected staff are not retained.

There are good reasons why organizations need to consider the reaction of applicants to selection methods. If the selection is viewed as the attraction of the organization may be diminished, candidates who have a negative experience can dissuade others, a negative selection experience can impact on job acceptance , selection methods are covered by legislation and regulations relating to discrimination, mistreatment during selection will put off future applicants and may also stop applicants from buying the organization's products or using their services.

- role of HR technology

What is the role of technology in Human Resource Development? Identify some key forms of e-learning and critically evaluate their advantages and disadvantages, providing appropriate examples from organisations. It will define what Human Resource Development is and why it needs technology. Also it will discuss what electronic learning (e-learning) is, and will explain some key forms of e-learning and why we need to use e-learning. It will give a brief indication as to what technology actually is, and also the progression of technology. The essay will critically evaluate the advantages and disadvantages of using e-learning in Human Resource Development. There will be appropriate examples used to show how different organisations use e-learning within their company/organisation. Finally it will offer conclusions as to why I think technology should or should not be a part of Human Resource Development.

Why does HR development need technology?

Technology is always progressing and this is very good for companies who need or even sell technology. If we look at how a few years back within companies the secretary would need to file documents manually and this could take a long time, also apart from the time issue there were more serious problems like documents going missing or being damaged. This is where technology began to progress because there was a new technology progressing and this was the database and this could hold all the documents you needed safely onto the computer and that way it would be a lot faster and more secure for the secretary to file the documents. This is just one example there are many more ways in which technology has helped to progress companies. The example given here is just to show that technology is progressing and it will keep progressing much further in the future years to come.

Human Resource Development is all about learning, training, developing and education the employees in the workplace. There is a difference between these four concepts but there all correlated. If for example we looked at learning; this can be learnt anywhere and you can be learning yourself the new skills, but on the other hand if you looked at education you are being taught something but in a formal way but the two are linked because from both of these you are learning new skills and then you can go on to training and developing them skills.

HRD was not always known as this, there was a shift from welfare officers to HRD. HRD was initially set up for training and development and this was to help the employers in crafts such as electricians, or engineers as an example and from this they would be learning from their masters and will be developing their skills to be able to perform in the workplace. HRD created an integration of people management and development and this could become CIPD which stands for the chartered institute of personnel and development.

HRD likes to be strategic and is more for the organisation than the employees; it is also a long term method to help to build the company. HRD does like to implement change into their methods and this is why e-learning will be very convenient to help within organisations because it is constantly changing and this change would help employees improve on their learning and training and will be able to implement new skills within the workplace.

Why does HR needs e-learning in organization? Firstly before I go into detail about how e-learning helps HRD perform you will need to know what e-learning actually is. E-learning used to be known as computer-based learning, this is basically what it still is, it is a way of learning but on a computer or even these days there is even m-learning which is through the mobile. We need e-learning in everyday life to be able to adapt the required skills in education, employment, even at home. It can be defined as any learning activity supported by information and communication technologies which is known as ICTs. There are arguments out there concerning the labels, an example of this is whether ICT-based learning is the same as e-learning, we can gather information from the world wide web channel and this would be our online materials, but we can also get materials from this intranet would could be confused as being from the world wide web but instead this material is delivered through an internal network of personal computers. E-learning is in fact taken to mean any form of electronic technology which can support learning this can be opposed to the chalk and blackboard technology which used to be the main form of learning.

- Why is HR strategy important to influence organizational success?

In organizational level, humans do formalize strategies as a function to direct and focus their efforts. However, in a business organizational (a firm), such efforts will focus on creating value for profit. In fact, the environment is a market with limited resources and therefore it causes competition exists. This environment mght be more or less stable, but it is in constant change.

HR Strategy will become a systemic and rational act, a process that can be managed in order to successfully attain in the golas of the firm. HR Strategy can divide these three kinds. Firstly, a HR plan is intended to achieve a particular purpose and to develop a HR strategy for dealing with unemployment. It is overall HR strategy to gain promotion. For government (public organization's economic HR strategy example. Secondly, it is the process of HR planning or putting a HR plan into operation in a skillful way. Finally, for war strategy, it is the skill of HR planning to be trained to the movements of armies in s battle or war. An example, of military HR training strategy, defend, strategies compare tactic.

However, nowadays, business organizations need " office of general", " command" , " generalship" skillful actions, leadership and leading welfare from one leader, such as CEO who have any effective HR strategy to manage staffs and tasks as well as leading them to serve their organizations successfully. So, an effective HR strategy can give good HR planning direction to let the organization to know whether it ought need how to do in order to achieve its HR development goals successfully.

An effective HR planning direction can achieve the organizaton's HR allocation goals more easily. For example, knowing how it can use of common resources (e.g. available human and technological resources). A basic HR strategic advantage tool win and prevail over rivals in the market comes from the differentiated used of such resources.

In beverage competitive industry example, Coca-Cola soft drink organization example, it was still keeping its predominance in the beverage market product " Coke", Pepsi Co was advancing fast on the base of a successful "image" HR strategy targeting the youngest segment of the beverage market under the taste of the new generation. So, it can select to employ more young workers to work in its organization in order to persuade many youngest soft drink customers to believe it is one young soft drink health drinking company. By 1983, Pepsi had begun to outsell coke in supermarkets when coke maintained its edge only through soda vending machines and fast food restaurants. Although, different marketing strategic breakthrough by far unexpected. It follows all time successful formula of coke. In 1985, the " New Coke" was introduced after an extensive study of market trended, surveys, focus group and taste tests strategies. In these survey investigation process, it must need to employ many part time or full time questionnaires staffs, they can include students, housewives, freelance workers, unemployed workers. So, HR department needs have enough time to select the right applicants to finish the whole questionnaire investigation project efficiently and effectively. The HR arrangement need to gather information to conclude this goals, such as how to design the new formula (or taste) was based on a different (lower cost) source of sugar, high fructose corn syrup to replace cane sugar. All of Coca (the plant from which comes the allealoid cocain) derivates were also removed from the old formula. So, how to design the taste is the main survey information gathering aim. Also, how HR arrangement which can have enough questionnaire staffs to carry on gathering information from the taste tests in the limited time to achieve to finish the taste test questionnaire project efficiently and effectively.

What are HR strategic benefits? They include: It can assist an organization to protect its HR capital base. It is a well accepted business principle, it can also help the organization to extend this notion to the world' natural and human resources, it can help leaders to plan and measure HR employment and reward and welfare and performance management systems of business enterprises more accurately, it can help business leaders to do the best balance between narrow self-interest and actions takes for the good of unemployment or creating more opportunity solution benefit in society as well as they can do actions in pursuit of financial survival more easily.

Why can HR strategy help organizational change in success? Knowing the importance and implication of organizational change and admitting the fact that organizational change success and leader / leadership can play a key role in bringing and implementing these changes by deciding the desired form of an organization and taking the potential steps which are needed for the process. So, when one organization has one good HR strategy, it can assist its organization to change more people and non-people resources effectively and efficiently.

Why do organizations need to change HR strategy? Nowadays, dynamic business environments influence organizations that respond quickly and effectively to constant change. A dynamic enterprise has two important tasks. It must adapt the current business environment, e.g. people skillful shortage in the industry into a shared HR strategy and then quickly and effectively to employ talent people or potential people to do the skillful job for its organization.

Reference

Andy, W.C. and Barry, J. B. and Wai, M.M. (2002) , Managing human resource in Hong Kong, Hong Kong: Thomson, p.6

Source: The harvard model of HRM

Beer , M., specter, B., Lawrence, PR. and Mills, D. Q. (1984). managing human assets. New York: Free press.

John, B. & Jeff, G. (6 edition, 2017). Human resource management theory and practice, Palgrave, Macmillan publishers ltd. UK , London,pp.4-5

John, H. (2013) managment a very short introduction, Oxford university press, UK, pp.11-13

Sources

http://info.shine.com/industry/automobiles-auto-ancillaries/2.html retrieved on 14 th May 2014

https://www.kpmg.de/docs/auto-survey.pdf retrieved on 17 the June 2014

CHAPTER FOUR

Training and Learning

What are the technique sector to solve above aspect of problems to HR?

John, A (2018) identified the major problems relate to HR personnel management, they include that selection of personal problem aspect, he explained that even if one knows precisely what qualities are required of man to do a given job well, it is still difficult to determine whether any given candidate has these qualities. On training problem aspect , he indicated that the cost of training staff is rapidly increasing, due largely to the increasing level of skill needed to operate modern equipment in the factory and office. Poor training will bring low earnings, high proportion of scrap production, mistakes, accidents results. Finally on salary and wage structure aspect, paid problems concern complaints of unfairness in the wage and salary differentials between levels of age, or skill, or between sections of the company.

What are the technique sector to solve above aspect of problems to HR? John, A (2018) explained that productivity bargaining, job evaluation, consultation and management by objectives techniques can be attempted to solve human relation problem; aptitude tests, intelligence tests, manpower planning, personality tests techniques can be attempted to solve selection of personal problem; needs analysis, programmed learning, business games techniques can be attempted to solve training problem; productive bargaining, job evaluation, merit rating, incentive schemes, salary progression curves, time span of discretion techniques can be attempted to solve salary and wage structure problem. John, A(2018) , he explained that how to apply the aptitude test to solve selecting personal problem. He assumed that increasing technology needs an ever larger number of skilled and semi-skilled employees in almost every field of industry , e.g. machines and processes are more complex to operate and maintain, computers must be programmed. However , training employees to the new higher standards is expensive and it is becoming increasingly important to select any those who will be able to reach the necessary standard. One way to determine whether a candidate will satisfactorily complete his training to be test his aptitude for the proposed task before his/her training starts these kinds of aptitude tests as below:

The technique consists of analyzing the physical and mental skills required to perform the task successfully and then estimating each candidate's aptitude in these by means of special tests. Typical examples of the testable skills are: manual desterity, ability to understand complex progress for chemical plant operators, mental aptitude for system analysis. Also standard training tests are now available for estimating certain aptitudes and where exist little training is required to give a test to a candidate. The training test is often a highly specialized job. Usually it will be able of someone in the personnel department to use this training test technique, but executives should be aware of its existence. Aptitude test advantage concerns buying a standard test is low, but the cost of having are specially prepared by an expert can be high. The training required to use them and interpret the results is slight. For some of the standard tests the correlation between those failing the test and failing a achieve the necessary standard of skill after training is good, i.e. substantial savings in training costs can be made by unsuitable candidates before spending money on their training.

John, A(2018) explained that how to apply brainstorming technique to generate new ideas. He assumes that new products have appeared on the market an ever-increasing rate, that is to say many product life-cycles are declining. So, new ideas in advertising in display in production technique to HR development is needed . Many companies are finding that their employees think creatively. They begin to the problem is that most employees not only fail to think creativity, but tend to use the old product, old market , outlets, old methods and old equipment for as long as possible habitually. He indicated that brainstorming strategy is a way of promoting new ideas. The usual method is for six to fifteen people need to meet for half an hour and propose answer to a question from the session leader. The questions may be that how many ways, we could increase sales of product (x), how many new market , we can think for product (y), in what ways we can redesign product(z). Hence, each member needs to present and they can be drawn from all levels and from any departments in the company. The leader speaks his/her idea to let the every member to listen and no one is permitted to criticize this idea, his/her idea provokes member to think of another.

Eventually, several ideas may be developed into one that is entirely new. Only when the session has ended do they start the rational process of determining whether the ideas can be practices or not. Then, any promising ideas can be subjected to " reverse brainstorming" in which the question in how many ways might this idea fail? is asked. Hence, brainstorming technique is good training to let staffs to create new idea method.

John ,A (2018) explained that intelligence test can be applied to select the right man for the job. he assumed that this problem of one of the requisites for any job is a minimum level of intelligence. How can this be measured? He explained that intelligence tests intelligence tests consist usually of a long list of questions to be answers and problems to solved within a set time. The number of questions answered correctly within this time is an indication of IQ of the candidate. Some training is required to apply an intelligence test to a candidate and to interpret the results, even when the test used is one of the well known standard ones.

How to design a test of this sort is a highly specialised job. All personnel officers should know about this technique and in large companies it may be desirable to train one officer in their use. Its advantages include cost is low, it only takes an hour or to test one candidate or a group of them. The effort is hotly debated. Without doubt these tests accurately measure IQ is a large proportion of cases.. In particular they can indicate whether a candidate has a very high or very high or very low IQ , although some doubt exists as to their accuracy in the middle ranges. However, the real debate concerns the accuracy of the results so much as their value. For IQ is said to be a measure only of a certain type of intelligence and not a guide to other types which may be more relevant to industry. Psychologists would certainly agree that an IQ test must be supported by an impression formed of the candidates ability in other ways, such as at an interview.

John , A(2018) indicated that a clear job description is needed to define what each employee is to do. In some companies , the employees have not been told exactly what their job is, with the result that sometimes two people attend to the same task neither knowing whose responsibility it is, or some task is not carried out at all, each man believing that someone else is attending to it.

In large organizations this can lead to cause the company has intense frustration and annoyance to individual employees. The job description technique is simple, the supervisor writes a description of each job, specifying each major activity as accurately as possible and limitations. Very little training is requires, but obviously it is necessary for someone with a fairly detailed knowledge of the company to draw up such descriptions. This is usually done by the supervisor of the job cooperation with the present job. It needs seldom take more than half an hour of two people's time to write out a fairly comprehensive description of any job. It's content may include job title , tasks , authority, superior, committees, limitations.

John, A (2018) explained that job evaluation is one effective method to select the right rate of pay for each job. He assumes that the all levels of wage or salary earners is the differential in rate of pay or between one job and another. How much more should the driver of a bus get than the conductor, how much most should a crane driver get than a fork life driver, how much more should a manager get than a foreman?

The first step in job evaluation is to carry out a job description for on can not evaluate a job unless each of several headings according to the requirements of the job. Headings according to the requirements of the job. Headings used often include such aspect as: skill needed to carry out the job, possible effects of careless number of months experience required to each proficiency, working conditions, including any unpleasant circumstances, such as excessive, temperatures or dustiness. Each job is evaluated in this way and then arranged in order of ascending total points into financial terms. For example, the dockside crane driver, process plant operator, canteen cleaner job's maximum points possible may include headings of skill (10), effect of carelessness (20), experience required (10) and working conditions (10) , maximum points possible.

John , A (2018) explained joint consultation is the effective method to improve human relations. He assumes that a large company feels junior employees who feel that nothing they can do will have any effect, and the top management is indifference to them or their happiness. The result is sometimes indiscipline and always indifference towards the company, its products, its reputation, its managers. Joint consultation is one effective employee engagement method , which is one way of drawing junior employees into the company and making them feel part of it is to allow them or encourage them to participate in management decision making or at least to discuss with them the consequences of management decisions. Many of decisions that managers take are highly technical and need great skill, long experiences and the use of time very advanced management techniques, e.g. capital expenditure appraisal is on such area. However, many decisions are more of a moral nature or affect employees more than they affect the company. Thus, joint consultation advantage can make a systematic attempt to consult with the employees to seek their opinions, ideas, reactions.

- What are on-job training advantages?

On -the-job training means that having a person learn a job by actually performing it. Virtually every employee, from mailroom clerk to company president, gets some on-the job training when he/she joins a firm. It usually involves assigning new employees to experiences workers or supervisors who then do the actual training.

Coaching or understudy method means that the employee is trained by an experienced worker or the trainee's supervisor. At lower levels, trainees may acquire skills for, e.g. running a machine is observed by the supervisor. Top management level, to the position of assistant is often used to train and develop the company's future top managers.

Job rotation, in which an employee usually a management trainee, moves from job to job at planned schedule. Special assignments similarly, give lower-level executives firsthand, experience in working on actual problems. Its advantages include relatively inexpensive trainees learn when producing and there is no need for expensive off-job facilities like classrooms or programmed learning devices. The method also facilities learning , since trainees are learned by actually doing the job and get quick feedback about the correctness of their performances.

Stages in training needs analysis includes as below: Preparation , deciding the objectives and scope of the training needs analysis; data collection is from employees in the real world; data analysis is needed to analyze the training needs in a systematic way; recommendation to propose the training budget, training design and evaluation methods; action is needed to identify the responsible person and time frame, and implement the plan,

Training principle means the effective motivation of the trainee is needed by the design of the training program and the methods which are used, the designing a training course is needed to consider the training requirements: attitudes, skills, knowledge. For example, a shop assistant in a convenience store, would require a certain friendly service attitude towards customers, skill in selling, displaying arrangement and knowledge of stock, sale procedures and the company's general policy.

On -the -job-training is given in the normal work situation, the trainee needs to use the actual tools, equipment, document, or materials, that he/she will use when fully trained. The trainee is regarded as a partly productive worker from the time training begins. Off-the-job training is taken away from the normal work situation, usually employing specially simplified tools and equipment. The trainee is not regarded as a productive worker from the beginning, it is exercise practice. Off-the-job training is needed to implement on the company's premises at a training center or at an educational institution.

On-the -job training advantages include that it is less costly because it uses normal equipment, the trainee is proficient, there is no transfer of learning problems, the trainee is in the production environment, he/she does not need to adjust to it after the less realistic conditions. Its disadvantages include the trainee may be a poor teacher and may not have enough time to give proper training, if there is a payment-by-results scheme, if may discourage the trainer from training, the training may be implemented in an inefficient way, a large amount of spoiled work and scrap material may be produced, valuable equipment may be damaged, the production conditions, which are stressful, i.e. noisy, busy, confusing, stress of this type usually inhibits learning. Otherwise, off-job-training advantages include the training is given by a specialist trainer and it should be of higher quality, special equipment, simplified of necessary can be used, the trainee can learn the job from easy to difficulty in planned stage, it is fee pressure of payment-by-work scheme, noise, danger, publicity, the trainee will learn correct methods from the beginning, the trainee does not damage valuable equipment or produce spoiled work or scrap, it is easier to calculate the cost of off-the -job training because it is more self contained. It's disadvantages include the higher costs of separate premises, equipment and trainers, learning difficulties to the trainee, when he/she needs to change training equipment to production equipment and a classroom environment to a production environment.

- The four steps of learning requirement

Any learning requirement include four steps: identifying the problem, seeking a solution, selecting an applying training and setting objectives. In seeking solutions steps, common performance problems and solutions include: lacks of skill problem can be solved to provide suitable skill training, insufficient knowledge problem can be solved by training to broaden understanding, lack of motivation problem can be solved by training might-enthuse, attitude problems can be solved by training of management commitment.

The important concern is that the training's topics and contents need to achieve this aim to improve employee (trainee) individual behavior, such as improvement of efficiency is concerned primary with doing things right, when effectiveness is about doing the right things well. Because highly efficient training courses do not mean that the training courses and contents are effective relevant to the company or individuals concerned needs.

Why does training need to set objectives? Because it can let the trainer gins a better understanding of the desired behaviors when it is seeking to encourage to achieve the training efficiently and effectively, let participants to know what the course details will help to overcome any uncertainty, and assist in motivating the individual and training objectives can indicate what the needs and requirements of the company. It can reduce the waste a quantifiable return on the time and capital invested before it has clear objectives for the training achievement.

Why does know what the main objective for training is more important? It has difference between aims and objectives. Aims mean to provide a direction or statement of intent. So, aim is at target, but the objective could be more clear. Whether this objective is realistic one would depend on the people involved and the circumstances under which they operate. This means that when an aim might express a desired outcome, it is the objective which will seek how and when this is attained or desired more easily. So, when the trainer can predict what (are) is the more accurate objective(s) , when this objective(s) is (are) confirmed the real need to the organization's benefit. The training will be more effective or avoids ineffective training consequence (irrelevant training courses and contents) to let trainees (participants) to learn, it means that time and money wasting of the training course.

David, L. (2016) explained that why a lesson plan is necessary. He indicated that " the existence of lesson plan can have positive effects. It depends on whether the methodology of knowledge (the how we do it) , but at this stage we are simply examining the knowledge itself (what knowledge are we trying to communicate). However, there are three principle classifications of information. Firstly information that the group must know, it means that there are items of information which are essential to the understanding of the topic in question. In most cases, they will have already been identified in any training need analysis and as they are fundamental to the success of any training course on the subject they must be given the highest priority. Secondly, information which trainers should know would include anything which related directly to the information in the must show category. For example, this might include other practices and procedures which interlink with those requires for safety reasons. Finally, the could know matters are those which can be described as useful to the group , but largely incident to the subject. These are items of information which , if time permits, could provide a useful background to the topic , but won't directly assist in its effective execution. This category would include historical details, boarder aspects, of the task, further areas of interest and general information."

The classification of information into these three categories allows each aspect of the subject to be examined and assigned to the appropriate category. In this way, it is possible to provide a degree of prioritization , enabling all the essential elements to be concerned in time available and any secondary information to be incorporated as and when circumstances permit.

However, these are number of other factors which will have an impact upon the structure topic and content of any training course . These include: level of understanding, course size, availability of equipment and material, financial constraints and timing. For example, a person's existing knowledge or cognitive inventory will influence whose level of understanding whether it is more or less easily when the trainee is learning the training course, the number of people participation will affect how much can be accomplished and what facilities and trainers are necessary for the course size arrangement, the availability of equipment and materials, e.g. what materials are needed and are available to avoid the kinds of equipment limited supply shortage, the financial constraints' aim to satisfy the course objectives at the lowest cost feasible, and achieve the highest standard of training possible at a cost that is acceptable to the organization. If the objectives of the course can't be achieved within the limits of available budget, then it is better not to run the course at all then to run unsuccessfully. Finally, the training course whether it has enough time to prepare all teaching arrangement to avoid bad or ineffective training consequence and not to cover-estimate what can accomplished during this period.

- Training and development steps

Gary, D. (2000) indicated that employee orientation provides new employees with basic background information, who need to perform their jobs satisfactorily , such as information about company rules. Orientation is actually part of the employer's new employee socialization process. Socialization is the ongoing process of researching in all employee the attitudes, standards, values, and patterns of behavior that are expected by the organization and its departments.

Training refers to the methods used to give new or present employees the skills, they need to perform their jobs. Training might mean showing how to operate its new methods, a new supervisor how to interview and appraise employees. Training is used to focus mostly on teaching technical skills, such as teachers devises lesson plans. However, technical training likes that is no longer sufficient. Employers have had to adapt to rapid technological changes, improve product and service quality and boost productivity to stay competitive. Improving quality (quality improvement programs) require employee who can produce charts and graphs and analyze data. Similarly, employees need skills (training) in team building, decision making, and communication, as well as technological and computer skills (such as desktop publishing, computer aided design and manufacturing) . And as competition demands better service, employees require customer service training for the tools and abilities require to serve customers.

Gary, D. (2000) also explains the five step training and development process, such as below:

First step is needs analysis, which identifies specific job performance skills needed to improve performance and productivity, analysing the audience to ensure that the program will be suited to their specific levels of education , experience and skills as well as their attitudes and personal motivations, using research to develop specific measurable knowledge and performance objectives.

Second step is instructional design, which gathers instructional objectives, methods, media description of and sequence of content examples, exercises and activities. Organizing them into a curriculum that supports adult learning theory and provides a blueprint for program development. Making sure all materials, such as video scripts, leaders' guides, and participants' work tools, complement each other are written clearly into the started learning objectives, carefully and professional handle all program elements, whether reproduced on paper, film or tape to ensure quality and effectiveness.

Third step is validation, which introduces and validates the training before a representative audience. Base final revisions on pilot results to ensure program effectiveness.

Fourth step is implementation, when applicable , boost success with a train-the-trainer workshop that focuses on presentation knowledge and skills in addition to training content.

Fifth step is evaluation and follow up, assess program success according to: reaction to document that learners' immediate reactions to the training, learning to use feedback devices or pre to measure what learners have actually learned, behavior to note supervisors' reactions to learners' performance following completion of the training. This is one way to measure the degree to which learners apply new skills and knowledge to their jobs, result to determine the level of improvement in job performance and assess needed maintenance.

- How to choose learning or training method

Methods of learning, training and development plans, training sources can be internal to the company or employees are trained from an external organization. Training can range from short term to long term, from online to in-person and from low cost to high cost development program for senior or specialist staff could learn techniques , such as coaching and mentoring or second, formal or off-the-job learning or educational arrangement.

The choice of learning methods depend on several factors include: the nature and degree of priority of the learning needs, type of occupation, level of seniority and qualifications/educational background of learners, organizational culture, evaluation of the effectiveness of previous learning and training results, experience, time required to complete training, learner preference, each individual may prefer learning in different ways, some prefer classroom learning over real-life practicing , learner preference's over learning ways and styles and their individual characteristics need to be taken into account when selecting , developing and delivering learning methods. For example, in-house courses provide an opportunity to focus on company specific issues. External courses involves interaction with people from other companies. For example, in-house, on the job training aims to deliver on a one-to-one basis at the trainee's place of work, allocated time to a specified , planned and structured activity.

Reference

David , L. (3 edition, 2016). The Group Trainer's
Handbook, Designing And Delivering Training For groups , Kogan Page , US pp. 18-19

Gary, D. (8 edition, 2000), Human resource management , Prentice hall, New Jersey.pp. 248-251

John, A. (2018) Management techniques, a practical guide, London, UK and New York , US: Routledge, pp. 27, 34-37, 67, 70-71,133, 140-144.

CHAPTER FIVE

PERFORMANCE MANAGEMENT

Pay structure steps

Human professionals might create the pay structure for their organization, or they might work with an external compensation consultant. There are several steps to design a pay structure: job analysis, job evaluation, pay survey analysis, pay policy and development and pay structure information (Milkovish, G., & Newman, J. 2008).

Milkovich, G. & Newman, J. (2008) explains that the pay structure steps include as below:

Step one : Job analysis is the process of studying jobs in an organization. The outcome of this process is a job description that includes the job title, a summary of the job tasks, adjust of the essential tasks and responsibilities and a description that includes the knowledge, skills and abilities needed to perform the job.

Step two: Job evaluation is the process of judging the relative worth of jobs in an organization. The outcome of job evaluation is the development of an internal structure or hierarchal ranking of jobs. Job-based evaluation is used more often than person-based evaluation and so the former will be the focus in this case. There are three methods of job-based evaluation: The point method, ranking and classification. The job evaluation helps to ensure that pay is internally worth perceived to be fair by employees.

Step three : Pay policy identification is the process of determining whether the organization wants to lead or meet the market in compensation. The pay policy or strategy will likely influence employee attraction. Pay policies can vary across families , i.e. groups of similar jobs, and job level of the top management feels that different areas of the organization.

Step four: Pay survey analysis is the process of analysising compensation data gathered from other employers in a survey of the relevant labor market. Gathering external data , e.g. base pay, bonuses , stock or share options and benefits is the essential to keep the organization's compensation externally competitive within the industry. Employee attraction can be improved by maintaining externally pay structures.

Step five: Pay structure creation is the final step, in which the internal structure (step two of job evaluation) is combined with the external market pay rates . Step four: Pay survey analysis in a simple regression to develop a market pay line. Depending on whether the organization wants to lead or meet the market, the market pay line can be adjusted top or down. To complete the pay structure , pay grades and pay ranges are developed.

In this organization's job analysis, it can influence these positions or job titles. For example, office support department has the lower level, front line receptionist, middle level, admin. assistant and top level, assistant to the director of operations. Operations department has the lower level, operations trainee, operations trainee, middle level , operations analyst, top level, director of regional operations, top level, director of regional operations. Human resource department has the lower level, payroll assistant, the middle level, benefits counselor and benefits manager, the top level, HR director.

In this organization, the administrative assistants, perform similar administrative tasks across departments and do not handle function-specific tasks , e.g. HR. Thus, this organization's administrative assistant ought be suggested grouping the front-line administrative jobs in a separate job family called office support. However, in some organizations, administrative assistant has possible to need to handle function-specific tasks, e.g. HR. Hence, in these organizations administrative assistant can be the low level group to HR department.

In the job evaluation step, this organization chooses to apply point method to evaluate the pay worth to every job title. The evaluation points method can be weights for example the four degrees for education level are identified as below:

1=high school, 2=assocaites, 3= bacholors, 4=master/graduate points are then calculated by multiplying the degree by the weights.

The compensable factor for the evaluation for front desk reception as below:

skill (50%) degree(1,2,3,4) weight points
education level 1 25% 25
degree of
technical skills 1 25% 25
responsibility(30%)
scope of control 1 10% 10
impact of job 2 20% 40
degree of
problem solving 1 10% 10
task complexity 1 10% 10
120

The ensure that the pay structure is extremely competitive, a pay survey will be conducted. The market pay data must be from the relevant labor market. Surveys can include i.e. six organizations who recruit and hire similar jobs in the regions. Base pay salary data from the responding organizations are reflected to ensure the summary job descriptions , sample data are appropriately similar to those in this organization in order to compare and analyze the pay data between other similar organizations and this organization.

Finally , it need to implement how to design the pay structure. it can be settled the pay ranges for each pay grade, pay ranges create upper and lower pay rates for each job in the pay scale. Each pay grade will have a minimum and maximum pay rate. It is important to remember that all jobs in a paygrade will have the same minimum and maximum pay rates. Percent guidelines below the midpoint the pay range will reach . For example, the maximum might be 10% percent above the midpoint and the minimum might be 10% below the midpoint. The percent guidelines can be based on input from the organization's job evaluation committee, e.g. clerical and office positions: 10% above and below the midpoint. Enter to mid-level professional and management positions: 30 % above and below the midpoint.

- What is key performance indicator (KPI) components?

Performance management strategy of performance metrics are a powerful tool of organizational change. It can measure organizational performance really. Companies define objectives , establish goals, measure progress, reward achievement, and display the results for all productivity. Executives can use performance metrics to define and communicate strategic objectives tailor to every individual and role in the organization. Managers can use them to identify forming individuals or teams and guide them and employees can use performance metrics to focus on what is important and help them achieve goal defined in their personal performance plans.

But wrong metrics can have unintended consequences: They can threaten to prolong on organizational processes, demoralize employees and undermine productivity and service levels. If the metrics do not accurately translate the company's strategy and goals into real useful actions that employees can take on a daily basis. Employees will work hard but have nothing to show for their efforts, everyone will feel tired and frustrated, also the company will be efficient but ineffective.

Performance metrics are a critical ingredient of performance management, performance management has a four steps cycle involves strategize misson, value, goals, objectives, incentives, strategy maps. Then, it needs to plan budgets, forecasts, models, targets. Next , it needs to monitor / analyze performance report, analytical tools. Finally, it needs to adjust or make action to assess, decide and track in execution step.

A performance metrics measurement tool can fasten the business, distill an organization's strategy to serve its stakeholders, linking strategy to processes. A performance metrics can give visual information delivery system that lets users measure, monitor, and manage the effectiveness of their tactics and their progress toward achieving strategic objectives . Collecting , a performance metrics measurement tool enable users to identify problems and opportunities, taken action and adjust plans and goals as needed.

What is key performance indicator (KPI) components? The only difference between a metric and KPA is that a KPI is a strategic objective and measures performance against a goal. KPI is a strategic objective . KPI measure performance against specific targets. Targets are defined in strategic planning, or budget sessions and can take different forms , e.g. achievement, reduction, absolute zero, targets have ranges of performance, e.g. above on, or below target. Targets are assigned time frame by which they must be accomplished. Time frame is often divided into smaller intervals, targets are measured against a baseline or benchmark. The previous year's results often serve as a benchmark.

The goals associated with KPIs are known as targets because they specify a measuerble outcome rather then a conceptual destination. Ideally, executives, managers and workers collectively set targets during strategic planning or budget discussions.

In performance management view point, target can be defined five types: Achievement means performance should reach or exceed the target. Anything over the target is valuable but not required, e.g. revenue and satisfaction. Reduction means performance should reach or be lower than the target. Anything less than the target is value, but not required, e.g. absolute means performance should equal the target. Anything above or below is not good, e.g. in-stock percentage and on time delivery. Minimum/maximum means performance should be within a range of value. Anything above or below the range is not good , e.g. mean time between repairs, zero means performance should equal zero, which is the minimum value possible, e.g. employee injuries and product defects. All above these target will be key performance indicator performance tool.

For time frames example, performance targets have time frames, which affects hoe KPIs are calculated and displayed. Many organizations establish annul targets for key processes. To keep employees on track to achieve those long -term targets, many organizations divide time frames into intervals, that are measured on a more frequent basis. For example, a group may divide the annual target to improve customer satisfaction from 60% to 68% into four quarterly inter with 2% target improvement each quarter. However, in some cases, such as a retail environment is affected by seasonal shopping, groups many back weighs. The targets toward the end of the year, since most holiday season, during the Dec. holiday season.

Finally, KPI targets could be measured against a benchmark that becomes the starting point for improving performance . Typically, the benchmark is last year's output. So, for example, a sales team may need to increase sales by 20% compared to last year. Or the benchmark could be an external standard , such as the performance level of an industry leader. So, a company might want to set a goals of closing the gap in market share with its closet competitor by 50% next year.

Users can read KPIs to look at a visual display that has been properly encoded and know whether a process of project is on track. To assist users can understand KPI (key performance indicator) performance measurement more easily. It has seven attributes for each. They include: status measures performance against the target and is usually shown with a stoplight. Trend measures performance against the prior interval or another time period and is often displayed using arrows or trend lines. The actual and target values are self-explanatory and usually displayed with text. Variance measures the gap between actual and target and is displayed using text or a micro bar chart in performance report variance percentage divides the variance against the target. These seven attributes can combine to provide valuable insight into the state of performance.

- How to Implement a Performance Management System

Depending on what kind of changes have been made we will have to prepare a communication and change management plan in order to transfer the organization smoothly from one to another PMS. While the small changes can be covered by simple communication informing about the changes in the system, major changes may even require change of mindset and old habits, which will need a more serious change management plan.

It is a system that is linked to and feeds many other HR tolls and systems meaning that the final results of those tools are highly dependent on the inputs that they get from the PMS. Having that kind of importance and influence this system, though complex in its nature, from one side has to be as simple as possible so that all managers can willingly and easily use it, while on the other side it has to offer quality results that can be used as inputs for the other HR tools and systems.

The quality of the system and the results it offers depend on the process of setting up the system itself. Doing a good job in planning, defining and introducing the system will do half of the job in securing quality results from the system. So how do we set up a Performance Management System?

Implementation of a Performance Management System is a project of its own... as every other project it needs serious approach towards all project elements and phases.

The implementation of a Performance Management System is a project of its own so it should be treated as one. So, as every other project of this character it needs serious approach towards all project elements and phases such as defining, planning, people, resource and stakeholder management, implementation, monitoring, measuring etc..

The performance management system may contain all of these components, but it is the overall system that matters, not the individual components. Many organizations have been able to develop effective performance management systems without all of the following practices.

A performance management system includes the following actions:

•Develop clear job descriptions using an employee recruitment plan that identifies the selection team.

•Recruit potential employees and select the most qualified to participate in interviews onsite.

•Conduct interviews to narrow down your pool of candidates.

•Hold multiple additional meetings, as needed, to get to know your candidates‘ strengths, weaknesses, and abilities to contribute what you need. Use potential employee testing and assignments where they make sense for the position that you are filling.

•Select appropriate people using a comprehensive employee selection process to identify the most qualified candidate who has the best cultural fit and job fit that you need.

•Offer your selected candidate the job and negotiate the terms and conditions of employment including salary, benefits, paid time off, and other organizational perks.

•Welcome the new employee to your organization.

•Provide effective new employee orientation, assign a mentor, and integrate your new employee into the organization and its culture.

•Negotiate requirements and accomplishment-based performance standards, outcomes, and measures between the employee and his or her new manager.

•Provide ongoing education and training as needed.

•Provide on-going coaching and feedback.
•Conduct quarterly performance development planning discussions.
•Design effective compensation and recognition systems that reward people for their ongoing contributions.
•Provide promotional/career development opportunities including lateral moves, transfers, and job shadowing for staff.
•Assist with exit interviews to understand WHY valued employees leave the organization.
•Performance Appraisals Don't Work tells you why you want to move away from the traditional appraisal system.
•Performance Management Glossary Entry provides a basic definition of performance management.
•Performance Management Is Not an Annual Appraisal provides the components of a performance management system.
•Performance Management Process Checklist gives you the components of the performance management process.
•Performance Development Planning provides the steps for preparing and implementing performance development planning.
•Performance Development Planning Form is used to write out specific goals and measurements, to be updated quarterly.
•Goal Setting: Beyond Traditional SMART Goals discusses goal setting.
•Tips to Help Managers Improve Performance Appraisals provides concrete suggestions about how those of you who have to manage in a traditional performance appraisal culture can make them better—for both you and the employee.
•Common Problems With Performance Appraisals identifies the most common reasons why appraisals are not effective.
•Phrases for Approaching Performance Reviews and Difficult Conversations shares tips about successfully holding a comfortable appraisal meeting.

Finally, performance appraisal is one part of performance management system. The process by which a manager or consultant (1) examines and evaluates an employee's work behavior by comparing it with preset standards, (2) documents the results of the comparison, and (3) uses the results to provide feedback to the employee to show where improvements are needed and why. Performance appraisals are employed to determine who needs what training, and who will be promoted, demoted, retained, or fired.

● Performance management aim

Performance management means the goal of reward programs are to attract, motivate people and it is essential for the company to clearly identify the performance and competency levels required of their employees in different roles at different levels. The company will then evaluate , differentiate and reward the employees in a fair and consistent way.

Performance management is one of the most important functions in human resource management. It is also an important tool to link individual objectives with departmental targets. It is a part of a comprehensive human resource management strategy. It needs to let objectives into practical and realistic performance goals at each level of the company. It provides employees clear aims and forms on job expectation motivates employees to perform better, helps focus on the desired results, improves communication, helps develop employees, capabilities and helps achieve organizational objectives.

It's elements include : planning means agreement on performance goals and targets, based on job descriptions and business objectives, goals and targets have to be specific to clear, measurable, specify quantity, quality, time, money etc., achievable to solve challenges, but within each of competent and committed person, relevant to the company's objectives. So, that the individual's goals can contribute towards the company's objective, monitoring and coaching means on ongoing and continuous process, monitor performance against agreed goals and targets, provide direction/ support and feedback on how well people are doing, recognize and reinforce desirable behaviours, coach and help solve difficulties in achieving desirable performance, identify problem at early stage, take corrective action in a timely manner.

Then, performance review or appraisal meeting means that it is a formal review on the individual's performance, it is usually done once or twice a year to review, monitor and employees for promotion, help identify the training and development needs of employees, achieve a better two way communication between the line manager and the employee with regards to performance.

Next, preparation for the appraisal meeting, it is necessary to keep a record of the individual's performance and achievement with gives support to rating, allow sufficient time for preparation on, what performance problems are to be mentioned, views on the possible reasons for success or failure, any suggestions to solve the problem, give sufficient notice to employee regarding the meeting and respect employee to have a self-appraisal before the meeting they can identify their own achievements and problems. Finally preparation of the appraisal form, it should be as simple and brief as possible and allow sufficient time for comments, terms should be easily understood, with some notes for guidance, information to collect on the form includes: Key result areas, agreed objectives/targets , assessment of performance against the key result area details of the development plan to improve performance.

What are the development activities participated for current appraisal period mean? Review the development activities are participated by the employee for the past appraisal period and to agree on a development plan for the coming appraisal period. Management coaching for performance means that managers and supervisors have an important role to play in performance management, which is to provide feedback and coaching on employee's performance when necessary, coaching is a process that helps the employee gain how to win overcome barriers to improve job performance on a as need basis, when training uses a structured design to provide the employees with the knowledge and skills to perform a task.

The other difference between coaching and training is that the former is normally done in real time. That is , it is performed on the job, at the workplace. The coach uses real-life tasks and problems to help the learners increase their performance. Otherwise, training and learning is taught to a group students to learn in a coaching is effective when it is specific to the individual and it is positive and it is positive and occurs as soon as performance problems are identifies.

Coaching for individual benefit performance includes to identify performance problem by pointing out the facts/ describing the behaviours observed in a professional manner, support with evidence if possible, clarify the expectations/standards of the job, explain the consequence of inappropriate actions/behaviours, ask for the employee's view point and how they assess their own actions/behaviours , discuss the causes of the problem/analyze reasons for sub-standard performance, develop and agree on solutions, decide on specific action(s) to be taken.

Why is reward communication important? for this case, a company could be wasting the money spent on salaries and benefits by leaving employees when they listen the true value of the total package. Without employee understanding, reward programs won't motivate employee effort reward achieving business objectives. So, effective reward communication can let candidates existing staff appreciate or understand the value of the retirement scheme or other benefits, such as subsidized meals, life insurance and critical illness insurance. However, if rewards are used to motivate employees, or to encourage higher performance aims, it is essential to have an effective communicating information about pay scales, the provision of benefits and allowances, grading systems, job evaluation , performance-related pay schemes and how pay decisions and made for different individuals or groups of employees.

In conclusion, performance management is not an annual appraisal meeting. It is not preparing for that appraisal meeting nor is it a self-evaluation. It's not a form nor is it a measuring tool although many organizations may use tools and forms to track goals and improvements, they are not the process of performance management.

Note: Performance management is the process of creating a work environment or setting in which people are enabled to perform to the best of their abilities.

Performance management is a whole work system that begins when a job is defined as needed. It ends when an employee leaves your organization. Performance management defines your interaction with an employee at every step of the way in between these major life cycle occurrences. Performance management makes every interaction opportunity with an employee into a learning occasion.

Performance management aims at building a high performance culture for both the individuals and the teams so that they jointly take the responsibility of improving the business processes on a continuous basis and at the same time raise the competence bar by upgrading their own skills within a leadership framework. Its focus is on enabling goal clarity for making people do the right things in the right time. It may be said that the main objective of a performance management system is to achieve the capacity of the employees to the full potential in favor of both the employee and the organization, by defining the expectations in terms of roles, responsibilities and accountabilities, required competencies and the expected behaviors.

The main goal of performance management is to ensure that the organization as a system and its subsystems work together in an integrated fashion for accomplishing optimum results or outcomes.

The major objectives of performance management are discussed below:

?To enable the employees towards achievement of superior standards of work performance.

?To help the employees in identifying the knowledge and skills required for performing the job efficiently as this would drive their focus towards performing the right task in the right way.

?Boosting the performance of the employees by encouraging employee empowerment, motivation and implementation of an effective reward mechanism.
?Promoting a two way system of communication between the supervisors and the employees for clarifying expectations about the roles and accountabilities, communicating the functional and organizational goals, providing a regular and a transparent feedback for improving employee performance and continuous coaching.
?Identifying the barriers to effective performance and resolving those barriers through constant monitoring, coaching and development interventions.
?Creating a basis for several administrative decisions strategic planning, succession planning, promotions and performance based payment.
?Promoting personal growth and advancement in the career of the employees by helping them in acquiring the desired knowledge and skills.

Some of the key concerns of a performance management system in an organization are:
?Concerned with the output (the results achieved), outcomes, processes required for reaching the results and also the inputs (knowledge, skills and attitudes).
?Concerned with measurement of results and review of progress in the achievement of set targets.
?Concerned with defining business plans in advance for shaping a successful future.
?Striving for continuous improvement and continuous development by creating a learning culture and an open system.
?Concerned with establishing a culture of trust and mutual understanding that fosters free flow of communication at all levels in matters such as clarification of expectations and sharing of information on the core values of an organization which binds the team together.
?Concerned with the provision of procedural fairness and transparency in the process of decision making.

The performance management approach has become an indispensable tool in the hands of the corporates as it ensures that the people uphold the corporate values and tread in the path of accomplishment of the ultimate corporate vision and mission. It is a forward looking process as it involves both the supervisor and also the employee in a process of joint planning and goal setting in the beginning of the year.

5.4 What is the difference between performance management and performance appraisal?

Performance appraisals are one of the crucial aspects of professionally managed organizations across the world. Each organization has set an appraisal system in place in order to raise its employees' performance over a period of time. They are based on a review of the performance of an employee on the tasks assigned to it. They are used for many aspects such as salary revision, bonus provisions, promotions etc. These reviews are mostly conducted annually, but may be considered quarterly or half-yearly as well depending upon the HR policies of the organizations. Mostly, Human Resource department takes the lead in conducting formal performance appraisals.

Otherwise, performance management systems are set in place to guide the employees to achieve a desired level of performance. It is basically a definition of what organization expects from employee over the next appraisal period. Specific objectives are set for short term (say next quarter), and employee is prepared to achieve the desired outcomes by meeting these short term targets. These targets are defined by the job description along with the desired outcome of the jobs. This helps employees to determine the gaps in their performance and thus helps them to improve before the final performance appraisal happens after a year or six months. However, performance management aims at overall personal development of the employees. It is a form of constructive feedback which encourages continuous improvement. It is helpful to both employee as well as appraiser. There is frequent communication between them which helps in setting right goals for the employee and possible guidelines from appraiser to achieve those goals in an effective manner. It therefore saves employees from the bitter feeling that comes at year end when they feel that they have wasted one whole year without any substantial value addition.

- What are performance management system

The common goals of performance management system consider our daily work routine about our purpose in an organization. It is important to let organizational members understand what their organizations' visions and goals are, how their work fits into the organization, and how they contribute to their mission accomplishment. Hence one effective performance management system can encourage and improve the organization's members to raise their effort to contribute to their organizations. So, it brings this question: How to design one effective performance management system?

A clear understanding of job expectations is needed. When employees and supervisors have a clear understanding of their specific job duties in the workforce are eliminated. Each employee will be expect to contribute their own duties and responsibilities efficiently. All effective performance management system can empower employees to think about and clarify every employee's role in the organization. Organizations need to set clear goals and expectations to help with them. Employee performance plans must provide for balanced, credible measuring expected results, the performance plans include results, the performance plans include appropriate resources, such as quality, quantity, timeliness, and/or cost-effectiveness. Moreover, performance expectations must be based on job analysis and understandable, reasonable and attainable and clear specific.

Regular feedback facilitates better communication in the workplace factor is important. Performance strengths and weaknesses. How can employee individual performance can get improvement? In fact, performance management can be a motivational tool, when this tool can let employees to feel more satisfactory. Then, the supervisors can have a performance feedback process that facilitates between the supervisors and their employees. Hence, performance feedback ought need to be regular feedback facilitated better communication in the workplace. It can reduce from normal pressures of work.

How to design effective performance management system ? AN effective management system can measure organizational and employee performance. Performance management involves multiple levels of analysis, and is clearly linked to the topics studied in strategy HRM as well as performance appraisal. The objectives of performance management system often include motivating performance, helping individuals, developing their skills, building a performance culture, determining who should be promoted, eliminating individuals who are poor performers, and helping implement strategies.

Hence, the main purposes of a performance include: The work is performed the best by employees, employees have a clear understanding of the quality of work expected from them, employees effectively these are performing relative to expectation, awards and salary increases based on employee performance are distributed, opportunity for employee development and finding reasons and solutions why the employee performance that does not need expectation. These issues will be performance management usually main purposes.

However, performance management system usually have these phases: Phase 1 (developing and planning performance) , It includes outline development plans, setting objectives and getting commitment for the organization. Phase 2 (managing and review performance), it includes assess against objectives, feedback, coaching , document reviews, . Phase 3 (reward performance) , it includes personal development, link to pay , results performance. What is the performance management aim? On setting objectives stage, the management needs to know how to achieve and help to encourage commitment and understanding by linking. The employees' work with the organization's goals and objectives. It needs to let employees to know how to achieve its missions clearly. So, targets need to be settled for each performance and goals setting is the fundamental aspect for an organization. They further indicated that productivity gains will be supported for and employees' participation in the process of setting objectives. It is a motivational process which also gives the individual the feeling of being involved and creates a sense of ownership for employees.

In management and review stage, this involves maintaining a positive approach to work, updating and revising initial objectives, performance standard and job competency areas as conditions change, requesting feedback from a supervisor, providing feedback to supervisors, suggesting career development experiences, employees and supervisors working together, managing the performance management process.

Hence, performance needs to be compared. It is between desired performance and actual performance. When they are measured , then they will give feedback and development. Then, feedback will five opinions to desired performance in order to make performance revision again, even again. Finally, when the desired performance can be achieved the best actual performance measurement result and it will bring actual performance development to achieve actual vision, mission, strategy, value drivers consequently.

IN the rewarding performance, it has three activities: personnel development, linking to pay and identifying the results or performance. In fact, all personnel development is basically self-development. Opportunity for development is valuable only if the individual capitalizes on himself/herself. Development should be designed to improve performance on the current job and then prepare the employee for promotion. In fact, it is only the employees who get promoted , who are currently doing outstanding work and this have been able to demonstrate their capacity to assume greater responsibilities. Furthermore, training activities should ideally to based on performance gaps that are identified during the performance review phase.

So, regular performance feedbacks are important factors to influence skills development. In addition organizations need a growing interest in pay-for -performance plans focused on small groups or teams. Small group pays provide monetary rewards based on the measured performance of the group or team. However, high performing, effective organizations have a culture that encourages employee involvement. Therefore, employees are more willing to get involved in decision-making, goal setting or problem solving activities, which subsequently result in higher employee performance.

Thus, one effective performance management system needs to follow these steps to implement, such as developing and planning performance step: it includes to set what the main objectives , the organization needs. Then it is managing and review performance step, the organizations need to review whether what differences are between its desired performance and actual performance to prepare review their performance difference. Next, it is reward management implementation, the organization needs to give better record to the talent employees in order to encourage they develop their skills in the maximum effort as well as it also needs to punish the poor performance employees in order to expect they can review their error. In consequence, all these steps must be followed step by step to implement the performance management system effectively.

Reference

Milkovich, G., & Newman, J. (2008). Compensation, MC Graw-Hill Irwin. 0*NET. Available at http://online.onetcenter.org

CHAPTER SIX

SOURCING AND STAFFING

- How to build talent staffing source

Marion, D. & Michel, S. (2014) explained talent is the sum of a person's abilities, his or her intrinsic grifts, skills, knowledge, experience, intelligence, judgement, attitude, character and drive. It also includes his or her ability to learn. At the international level, talent shortages are more severe. During the past decade, an internationally mobile group of employees, who can pick and choose where they work. As firms in employing markets also begin competing in the global economy, these people are in ever-greater demand. For example, Singapore has had on an intensive recruitment program for skilled foreign workers, with more liberal criteria for eligibility to work in the country. Some 90,000 now work in the city-state, the majority from the US, UK, France, Australia, Japan and South Korea.

Marion, D. & Michel, S. (2014) indicated several factors need to be taken into account to understand the market for skilled labour. Hays and Oxford Economics pooled their data to identify seven components that together give a better picture of skill shortages as below:

Labour-market participation means the degree to which a country's talent pool is fully utilized, for example, whether women and older workers have access to jobs; labour -market flexibility means the legal and regulatory environment is faced by business, especially how easily immigrants can fill talent gaps; wage pressure overall means whether real wages are keeping pace with inflation; wage pressure in high-skill industries means which wages in high-skill industries outpace those in low-skill industries; wage pressure in high-skill occupations means rises in wages for highly skilled workers are a short -term indicaton of skills shortages, talent mismatches means the mismatch between the skills are needed by businesses and those available, are indicated by the number of long-term unemployed and job vacancies; educational flexibility means whether the educational system can adapt to meet the future needs of organizations for talent, especially in the fields of mathematics and science.

Firms operating in knowledge-intensive industries depend on their most capable staff to help create value through intangible assets, such as patents, licence and technical know-how. In fact, globalisation and technological competition brings to much complexity of many jobs and occupations. Firms are now looking for individuals with an range of abilities that might include specialized skills, broader functional skills, industry expertise and knowledge of specific geographical markets. The skills include: digital skill means the fast growing digital economy is increasing the demand for highly skilled technical workers. Companies are looking for staff with social-media based skills, especially in " digital expression". Agile thinking means the regulatory and environment uncertainty, such as life sciences and energy and mining industry's talent knowledge, ability skill is needed for employee's personal effort and characteristic needs; interpersonal and communication skill, H R managers predict that co-creativity and brainstorming skills be greatly in demand, it will bring relationship building and teamwork skills; global operating skill means that ability to manage diverse employee is seen as the most important global operating skill,, glocalisation (where home-market products and services are tailored to the taste of overseas customers and innovation (where staffs lead innovation and then the company applies these new ideas to mature markets).

Talent is a relative concept, it includes these components, such as technical specialists, especially in areas key to the organization's core capabilities, individuals with hard-to-recruit skills, bright individuals from underrepresented groups whom the positions , the best-performing graduates or school leavers and managers with the potential to move into senior management positions at the local, national or international level. However, judgement effort is the main factor to influence organizations to select individuals whose behavior and values fit with those of the organization. How performance and potential are measured is for senior managers to decide.

In many cases, the definition of exceptional performance is explained in competency frameworks and appraisal systems. Defining high potential can be more difficult and might include a range of assessment tools, such as development centers, psychometric testing and the personal judgement of those whose insights into talent are widely respected.

Talent plan has three components: talent gaps mean HR works with business management levels. Once a year to identify which leadership , management and functional skills are needed, how those roles and responsibilities and whether the talent processes are producing people who will be able to solve these skill gaps; talent supply means most of the focus is on management trainees and a smaller proportion of people who are recruited mid-career; talent development means recruiting high-potential individuals at the start of their careers and taking them through a structured development program.

Talent strategy means how senior leaders can identify the capabilities that help achieve the company's strategy strategic objectives and provide a competitive effort. These capabilities are not just tactical or operational skills, which although important, do have as much of an impact on business performance and profit. Operational management or senior levels and the talent management team then break down each capabilities into parts, such as specific skills, knowledge and expertise. They look at how these skills sets enable each business unit to deliver their part of the strategic plan.

This analysis should indicate the roles where knowledge and expertise are needed for maximum business value. There are not automatically senior leadership or management values. They also extend to technical and specialist roles or to previously overlooked roles, e.g. positions within the organization that help sure that expertise from one part of the business. Part of review many necessitate a fresh look at knowledge management processes across the business. The HR team should also review its own ways of working and thinking o make sure that its processes for recruitment, selection, learning and development, appraisal , reward and recognition and concentrates on the skills, cultural values and behaviors most critical to business performance.

Talent review aims to assess how well employees are performing currently in the critical roles, identified by the strategic review, and their potential to move into more demanding roles. Some of the required data will be held centrally by HR, but almost certainly, the team carrying out the review will need to speak directly to operational and line managers to get feedback about the performance and potential of key individuals.

At part of the review, gap analysis will help identify gaps in skills necessary to carry out the business's strategy and plans and whether any critical roles are unfilled. Succession planning is a important factor here as it may well be that insufficient numbers of potential successors have been identified for certain critical roles. A talent based gap analysis main aim is to focus on hiring and/or training needs as part of a talent strategy, it is the company's strategic planning process. It draws ona wide source of data, both internally and externally. It looks at strategic needs both current and future, and makes judgements about operational needs.

This analysis determines whether the right talented people are in the right position at the right time. These three factors will influence whether talent planning needs to be improved. For example, right people, but wrong time, it means that people who might not be being used currently because of ao downturn in markets, but who the organization does not want to lose as it takes too much time and money to replace them when demand increases. The organization must therefore determine its strategy for retaining and motivating them; wrong people means that people are not employed to perform the work .

This suggests that a mistake is between HR processes and the business strategy, learning and development processes may not be keeped good with changing business needs. There may be needed to appraise and promote to make right decisions that are leading to a mismatch between roles and people, right people, but wrong location. It means that people who can do the work , but are in the wrong location as a result of a reorganization and constraints on mobility, make more creative use of temporary assignments and virtual working, or relocate work to where it can be done by the most skilful employees.

Finally, once the talent review has identified any shortagesof talent, an organization has three options: either buying talent through external recuritment or building talent through tailored learning and development programmes that involve work experiences that will help talent employment development or borrowing talent by resorting to temporary workers or outsourcing.

Buying talent is an obvious choice when a company needs particular skills or expertise that it does not have time or ability ro develop in existing staff is to buy in that talent. The task is then to source this expertise, and offer the right set of inducements to recruit and retain individuals with the desired skills. However, buying talent can be costly as the going rate for sought-after specialists is high and they are often in a strong negotiating position. For example, swift recuritment processes and flexible remuneration package can attract talent employees' applications through external recuritment seeking recritment method.

Borrowing talent is a temporary need for specialist skills it makes sense to borrow or " rent" what is required by contracting with, for example, freelancers, independent consultants, staff on seondment or firms that will supply staff. This form of flexible labour means uncertain times such flexibility becomes more attractive because it enables firms to assemble new combinatins of skills in swift reponse to sudden shifts in their environment. It provides firms with access to wider pool of talent, especially in the case of work that can be performed in any location.

This, building talent means that a larger firm will seek to build its own talent by creating a reliable high potential and high performing employees. The aim is to rise and train talent skilful employees' qualities and efforts and to invest in their careers in the expectation that they will progress to senior positions in the business. So, these individuals are placed in a talent pool where their progress is monitored and where they are given extra opportunities for training and development. To keep talented people to develop, there is an emphasis on performance management, so any weaknesses or developments are needed to find.

- sourcing staff methods

Internal sources advantages of filling a vacancy internally, they include better motivation because employee capabilities are more ensured to promote or transfer, improved moral, performance and loyalty to the employee, lower staff turnover rate, better utilisation of employees because he/she owns more abilities in a different job or capacity , less training required, greater reliability than external recruitment because a present employee is the terms of personality, attitudes, values, work habits etc. known more, being quicker and cheaper than external recruitment. External source advantages when the company need to expand and growth contribute to the need for recruitment. Other factors include resignation, dismissal, retirement and relocation. Although internal recruitment has many advantages, many positions are filled by external applicants. When an internal candidate is transferred or promoted, it means that his/her position then because a vacancy, presuming that there is no reduction in staff numbers and no organizational restructuring. Hence, external recruitment can be time consuming , expensive and uncertain. However, organizations still need to conduct the external sources selecting method on a regular basis. The external recruitment source channels may include internal online or newspaper advertising, private employment agencies, professional bodies appointment services, local employment services office of government labor department, direct links with universities, colleges and schools, unsolicited applications, recommendations by present employees or by other employers' referrals.

Talent management steps in validating a test. Test aims to ensure whether the test listening and speaking competence, he/she owns the skillful effort is enough to do the vacancy or position in the organization. The steps in validating a test is as below:

The organization needs to analyze the job. It is necessary to conduct a careful job analysis to produce a good job description and an appropriate job specification. These requirements can then become the objectives of the selection tests. Then, it needs to choose the test from among the various testing means, choose the one that is the most valid and reliable. Next, it needs to administer the test. One can either test current employees and find out of there is any

significant differences between the scores and the employees' performances , it means concurrent validation or test potential candidates before they are hired and compare their scores with their performances after they have been in their jobs, it means predictive validation.
However, predictive validation may have disadvantages, e.g. job performance may be difficult to assess objectively, the process of validation may be lengthy, the results of the test are compared with the performance of a selected group only, it is not completely validated. Concurrent validation is quick, but its disadvantages may include standardisation is difficult, the test is validated against a non-typical group only, i.e. present employers rather than candidates for employment, the present employee may not behave normally when they do the test.

Reference

Marion, D. & Michel, S. (2014) the economist, Managing talent, Profile books ltd, London, UK, pp.1-2, 6.

CHAPTER SEVEN

EMPLOYEE ENGAGEMENT

employee engagement aim

What is employee engagement? The term employee engagement needs to be clearly understood by every organization. Some organizations perceive it as job satisfaction others say it's the emotional attachment towards the organization. Employee Engagement is a fundamental concept in the effort to understand and describe, both qualitatively and quantitatively, the nature of the relationship between an organization and its employees. An "engaged employee" is defined as one who is fully absorbed by and enthusiastic about their work and takes positive action to further the organization's reputation and interests. An engaged employee has a positive attitude towards the organization and its values.

An organization with "high" employee engagement might therefore be expected to outperform those with "low" employee engagement. Employee engagement improves the productivity of an organization as the practice helps the employees in teamwork, co-ordination and inter-personal skills. It means that such as morale and job satisfaction. Despite academic critiques, employee-engagement practices are well established in the management of human resources and of internal communications. Employee engagement today has become synonymous with terms like 'employee experience' and 'employee satisfaction'. The relevance is much more due to the vast majority of new generation professionals in the workforce who have a higher propensity to be 'distracted' and 'disengaged' at work.

The workplace environment impacts employee morale, productivity and engagement - both positively and negatively. The work place environment in a majority of industry is unsafe and unhealthy. These includes poorly designed workstations, unsuitable furniture, lack of ventilation, inappropriate lighting, excessive noise, insufficient safety measures in fire emergencies and lack of personal protective equipment. People working in such environment are prone to occupational disease and it impacts on employee's performance. Thus productivity is decreased due to the workplace environment. It is the quality of the employee's workplace environment that most impacts on their level of motivation and subsequent performance. How well they engage with the organization, especially with their immediate environment, influences to a great extent their error rate, level of innovation and collaboration with other employees,

absenteeism and ultimately, how long they stay in the job. Creating a work environment in which employees are productive is essential to increased profits for your organization, corporation or small business. The relationship between work, the workplace and the tools of work, workplace becomes an integral part of work itself. The management that dictate how, exactly, to maximize employee productivity
center around two major areas of focus: personal motivation and the infrastructure of the work environment.

In today's competitive business environment, organizations can no longer afford to waste the potential of their workforce. There are key factors in the employee's workplace environment that impact greatly on
their level of motivation and performance. The workplace environment that is set in place impacts employee morale, productivity and engagement - both positively and negatively. It is not just coincidence that new programs addressing lifestyle changes, work/life balance, health and fitness - previously not
considered key benefits - are now primary considerations of potential employees, and common practices among the most admired companies.

In an effort to motivate workers, firms have implemented a number of practices such as performance based pay, employment security agreements, practices to help balance work and family, as well as various forms of information sharing. In addition to motivation, workers need the skills and ability to do
their job effectively. And for many firms, training the worker has become a necessary input into the production process.

THE PROBLEM STATEMENT

The work place environment in a majority of industry is unsafe and unhealthy. These includes poorly designed workstations, unsuitable furniture, lack of ventilation, inappropriate lighting, excessive noise,
insufficient safety measures in fire emergencies and lack of personal protective equipment. People working in such environment are prone to occupational disease and it impacts on employee's performance. Thus productivity is decreased due to the workplace environment. It is a wide industrial
area where the employees are facing a serious problem in their work place like environmental and physical factors. So it is difficult to provide facilities to increase their performance level. Thus, effective employee engagement strategy can assist the organization's employees feel they are the organization's important members to serve their organizations to work more hardly in order to raise productivities easily.

- What is employee welfare mean?

Employee welfare includes everything, such as facilities, benefits and services, that an employer provides or does to ensure comfort of the employees. Good welfare helps to motivate employees and ensure increased productivity.
Providing good welfare to employees may be a costly decision, but the long-term benefits are immense. It is one way of complying with the law, thus ensuring that an employer avoids legal issues. It allows accompany to retain its good and skilled employees for long periods of time. Employees work well in workplaces where they are treated well and

respected. Good welfare also helps to create a good company image for a particular employer.

Employee welfare facilities in the organization affects on the behavior of the employees as well as on the productivity of the organization. While getting work done through employees the management must provide required good facilities to all employees.

The management should provide required good facilities to all employees in such way that employees become satisfied and they work harder and more efficiently and more effectively.

Welfare is a broad concept referring to a state of living of an individual or a group, in a desirable relationship with the total environment – ecological economic and social. It aims at social development by such means as social legislation, social reform social service, social work, social action. The object of economics welfare is to promote economic production and productivity and through development by increasing equitable distribution. Labour welfare is an area of social welfare conceptually and operationally.

It covers a broad field and connotes a state of well being, happiness, satisfaction, conservation and development of human resources

Employee welfare is an area of social welfare conceptually and operationally. It covers a broad field and connotes a state of well being, happiness, satisfaction, conservation and development of human resources and also helps to motivation of employee. The basic propose of employee welfare is to enrich the life of employees and to keep them happy and conducted. Welfare measures may be both Statutory and Non statutory laws require the employer to extend certain benefits to employees in addition to wages or salaries.

Labour Welfare Measures

Labor welfare includes various facilities, services and amenities provided to workers for improving their health, efficiency, economic betterment and social status.

Welfare measures are in addition to regular wages and other economic benefits available to workers due to legal provisions and collective bargaining. The purpose of labor welfare is to bring about the development of the whole personality of the workers to make a better workforce. The very logic behind providing welfare schemes is to create efficient, healthy, loyal and satisfied labor force for the organization. The purpose of providing such facilities is to make their work life better and also to raise their standard of living.

- Measurement the level of employee engagement factor

There are a number of external and internal factors that help measure the level of employee engagement. External factors include organization environment; its culture and values, manager-subordinate relationship, relationships with co-workers, monetary benefits and appraisals. Whereas internal factors include the personal values of employee, personality type and commitment to work. Gallup's research on employee engagement shows that there is a strong relationship between well being of an employee and the level of their engagement. An engaged employee is efficient an effective for the organizational outcomes.

Employee engagement has direct effect on productivity and growth. If employees are engaged they will try level best to fulfill their job responsibilities which will consequently lead to not only increase in organization productivity but will also enhance the self performance of employee. In the world of globalization only those organizations which have highly engaged workers can survive and grow. But an organization can engage its employees only if the employees have the desired attitude. Therefore an organization should train its employees to change their attitudes if they want to properly manage workforce engagement.

● employee engagement survey reasons

Nowadays, increasing diverse and geographically workforces bring global competition to live nd retain qualified employees aim. Organizations need to attract, motivately and engage employees though not only the core HR functions of compensation, benefits, performance management and talent development, but engagement programs, such as work life effectiveness, recognition and reward systems.

In fact, one strategic employee engagement if designed correctly, is cost-effective program and valuable tools that can measured and increase employee involvement and ethusiasm in their work and contributions to their employer's goals or values. Industry research analysts indicated that companies in the top employee engagement designed program, which can brough 16% higher profits and 18% higher productivity in general. They also evaluated the relationship between employee engagement and employee turnover. Companies with light effective recognition engagement programs have 31 % lower ineffective turnover than organizations with ineffective recognition programs. However, to be most impactful engagement solutions require innovative features to enble full service, effective management of strategic engagement programs. Social communicative elements along with rich analytics and mobile capabilities that interoperate with existing HR solutions are necessary to keep more efficient and effective changing HR needs and organizational goals.

As the economy slowly makes its way back in recovery mode and more employees are concerned with issues beyond job security. So organizations need to concern how to a focus on employee engagement and the criticial factor ithin organizations that drives performance. HR conulting forms point out a relationship between high levels of engagement and high levels of financial performance. Achieving overall employee engagement is overview to have need. For years, companies around the globle have conducted employee engagement surveys in an effort to determine why their organizations function the way they do, and how they can pull organizations to improve performance. The results of there employee engagement surveys sometimes reflect, better and accurate key business decisions and impacting the day-for-day lives of employees, shareholders and customers.

But is that really all these is to real reflection? Should company focus on employee engagement as the key indicator of success or failure within their organization? Is high employee engagement brings some sort of better management skills? It is absolute no answer. When employee engagement should be measured as an important organizations human resource and social system, truly understanding how to optimize performance in your organization requires understanding your organization requires understanding your culture. For example, we know that with some people, we can increase their engagement and satisfaction by simply, making their work easy-opertating in a go along to get along manner and more generally encouraging passive behaviors.

Employee engagement becomes a popular topic of the workplace instead of job satisfaction and organizational commitment which is approved to effect the organizational outcome. In HR department behaviors that affect th structured interviews were conducted in corporate HR to explore the employee engagement and techniques for improving employee engagement were recommended based on the interview.

The quantitative research results show that job autonomy , performance feedback, challenging work, worker person fit, development support and the connection with co-workers have a strong relationship with employee engagement. And the recommended solutions like building on action team, have more team activities and develop a formal both for big team (corporate HR) and smaller team will improve their engagement over time.

Organizations need to increase their performance by both efficiency and productivity. Managers would hardly deny that employees make a criticial difference in innovation, organization performance, competitiveness and lead to the business success. Hence, HR plays an important role in the employee engagement program with the responsibilities of the survey, providing feedback on results, prommoting communication in different groups of people, encouraging people to take action and providing educational opportunities. Employees growth, teamwork mangement support and basic needs are needed to measure by relevant questions in viewpoint survey by using five point scale. Personal growth is measured by talking about the progress and having job opportunity grow. The options count, mission and purpose fellow employees who committed to quality work and having a best friend at work and identified as the questions for measuring team work . Management support is measured by opportunity to do the best , recognition or praise care and encourage the development.

Employee survey can reflect employees engagement , e.g. one viewpoint survey for the past three years and every time survey has chance to let employees fill the survey in, then HR managers can get the results to give scores. Managers should take get move real feedback from different department staff's positive or negative emotion or feeling aboug whose job tasks, whether they worry about any job difficulties. Hence, surveys can let organizations try to figure out of their employees are engaged and how to make them engaged by using different surveys and tools to stay competitive and improve performance.

In survey contents, there are four main topics in the engagement survey: growth, teamwork, managment support and basic needs. The result can show the most items in engagement support were scored relatively low or high as mean of development support from manager. Hence, many organizations were focusing on designing a successful reward system to keep employees engaged and productive line or the low level managers who can serve their employees are typically the ones who work or fail the engagement tools because line managers need often communicate and contact workers when they are working. They can know what their feeling to their job tasks whether it is positive or negative emotion in order to find solutions how to raise their performance.

CHAPTER EIGHT

THE RELATIONSHIP BETWEEN HUMAN RESOURCE STRATEGY AND CORPORATE STRATEGY

In my opinion, it is very important how to implement one effective human resource (HR) management strategy, such as the development, award (compensation) management, learning and training (talent mangement), job evaluation (performance management review or appraisal, selection and recruitment activities. Because if the organization can achieve one effective HR strategic plan, then it will influence its organizatinal corporate strategy to achieve more successful. Otherwise, if it can not implement on effective HR strategy, then it will not influence its organizational corporate strategy to achieve more successful. I shall give my opinion to explain as below:

Ong Teong, W (2010) explained that one organization hopes to acvieve corporate strategic success. It needs to implement a result-management system to achieve results through and with people. The steps include: The first step is strategic focus: product/service delivery process, operation process flow, functional analysis, performance expectations and operation manual elements. Then second step , it divides two channels. The first channel is from stragic focus to achieve employee performance result as well as the another channel is to plan the management management(expectation), it includes: keu results areas, key performance indicates and target elements of action plans.

Then, it will implement the third step of performance management and review, it includes: evaluation: motivating, communication, coaching and counseling. Next it will bring two channels to the fourth step, the first channel is either it brings control to implement the performance appraisal and the performance appraisal stemp will give feedback to the first step of strategic focus again as well as the another channel is to give feedback to performance measurement second step again.

Thus, in consequence, operations manual, performance measurement, performance management and review and performance appraisal four steps will need to give feedback to achieve the employee performance final result step. So, the author indicated the whole results-measurement system whether it can achieve effective or non-effective employee performance result. It depends on how its first step of strategic focus implement plan to achieve either effective or non-effective performance measurement step, performance management and review step and performance appraisal step in order to achieve an effective or ineffective employee performance result or aim. So, it seens that one organization hopes to achieve excellent employee performance result or aim, the corporate's strategic focus will influence how it can plan one good results-management system to achieve good results through and with people. Thus, the organization's first step how to plan strategic focus, this step is very important to influence how it can bring either excellent employee performance result or poor employee performance result.

What is the strategic focus mean? It can be explained as to predetermine the ner term course of action and direct all business processes and functional activities to the collective priority of the organization for the year as a mangerial planning function. Expected organizational key results areas are also made known. So if the organization can predetermine that whether it ought how to do action and follow the correct directions to implement its functional activities to all business processes. It will bring effective human resource strategic plan to implement to achieve excellent employee performance result. Otherwise, if the organization cn not predetermine that whether it ought how to do action and follow the wrong directions to implement its functional activities to all business processes. It will not bring effective human resource strategic plan to implement to achieve excellent employee performance result. Thus, direct directions to strategic focus plan is a important factor to influence the organization's human resource strategic plan success in order to achieve either excellent employee performance result or poor employee performance result.

How can human resource management influence to strategic focus ? HRM can be defined: hiring and developing employees, so that they become more valuable to influence the organization's strategic focus whether it is success or fail. HRM includes: conducting job analyses, planning personnel needs, and recruitment, selecting the right people for the jobs, orienting and training, determining and managing wages and salaries, providing benefits and incentives, appraising performance, resolving disputes and communication with all employees at al levels. Som these elements will influence whether the organization can bring either excellent employee performance result or poor employee performance result.

Why does knowledge management can improve some organizations' employee performance to be better? Knowledge management is about developing, sharing and applying knowledge within the organization to gain a competitive advantage. It has argued that knowledge is dependent on people, and that HRM activities , such as recruitment and selection, education and development, performance management and pay/rewards as well as the creation of a learning culture are important for managing knowledge within organizations.

However, knowledge is either explicit or implicit. In this classification , explicit knowledge is considered to be formal and objective, and can be numbers and specifications. It can therefore be transferred via formal and systematic methods in the form of rules, procedures. Otherwise, implicit knowledge is subjective, situational , and is tied to the knower's experience. This makes it difficult to formalize, document and communicate to others. Insights, personal beliefs and skills and using a rule to solve a complex problem are example of implicit knowlege, such as learning computer software designing knowledge is one kind of implicit knowledge. So, implicit knowledge can be shared in relational situations, such as mentorships, and coaching and through in-house trainings, where experienced employees are encouraged to share their experiences with their colleagees.

In one organization, knowledge management is needed to let its employee to understand such as: what an organization knows, the location of knowledge , e.g. in the mind of a expert, e.g. computer software designing trainer in a specific computer software designing department, in old files' records, with a specific team etc. in what form this knowledge is stored, in the minds of experts, such as one computer software designing company's computer software designing trainers' minds, on paper, in notes of how to write the kind of computer software programme, how to best transfer this knowledge to the relevant people, e.g. the computer software designing trainees in order to take advantage of it and ensure that it is not lost, e.g. the kind of computer software designing skill and the need to methodically assess the organization's actual know-how versus the organiation's needs and to act accordingly, e.g. how to select to hire the most suitable employee to do the position, or how to follow the rules to promote specific in-house knowledge creation. Thus, knowledge management is useful or helping to any organization's employee skillful development because it focuses on knowledge as an actual asset, rather than as something intangible. If the organization can transfer its any knowledge to be actual asset, it enables an organization to better protect and exploit what it knows , and to improve and focus its knowledge-development efforts to match its needs.

I shall indicate computer software product manufacturing industry, knowledge management is important to influence the computer software company's software sale number. For example, computer software design industy, any computer software design organization ought need have good knowledge management strategy to improve its computer software designing programmer individual skill level to be upgraded in order to raise their every one computer software design programme skill. Thus, learning and training strategic plan is very important to computer software sale company's software design programmers or trainees). The computer software design trainer need have more

working experience to design software program and the high educational level for computer software designing program course if they want to be the trainers in any computer software companies in order to apply their computer software programming design skill or knowledge level to teach different different kinds of unique computer software design program knowledge concepts and theories and programming skill in order to let their computer software designing program trainees who can learn how to create different kinds of new and unique computer software products to cope further unpredictive different kinds of computer software product users

needs.

Thus, such as computer software program designing organization case example, it explains that why strategic focus can influence its employee performance, such as computer software programmer. If the computer software program designing organization can have one effective strategic focus or corporate strategic plan, how to process of formulating, implementing and evaluating business strategies to achieve organizational objectives, e.g. it's human resource of computer software program designing trainee training aim is that how to apply computer software design program knowledge concept and computer software program designing trainers know how to transfer their computer software design knowledge skills to their trainees easily in order to improve their computer software design knowledge to create and innovate the unique computer software to satisfy its further computer software product buyers' needs. Thus, when it have right or correct directions , e.g. how to teach its computer software program designing trainees to design unique computer software products to cope computer software buyers' needs. Then, its computer sodtware trainees will have more computer software program designing knowledge concept thinking to solve any computer software program designing problem, doing the most right methods or decisions makings to design computer software products innovations, taking risks and facing uncertainty to adopted the unpredictive further computer software product buyer individual need more easily. So, knowledge management skill to computer software program designing trainers which is very important to influence whether the kinds of computer software products are popular to accept to use for the computer software company. Also, it implies that when the computer software company has a right or correct strategic focus implement plan, then it will bring the correct or right knowledge management training courses to suggest its computer software trainers to know whether they ought how to teach or train their computer software trainees in order to imprive their computer software program designing skills effectively in order to satisfy its further unpredictive computer software company clients or individual computer software users their needs more attractively in the global competitive computer software sale market.

Thus, in computer software sale industry, training and learning strategy is one important part of human resource strategy to any computer software sale companies nowadays. Because computer software consumers had been often changing different kinds of computer software products' demands, they need to raise their software qualities to satisfy their needs. If the computer software company has none any excellent computer software programmers to design any new and unique computer software products to satisfy further unpredictive computer software product users' changing needs. Then, they can choose to buy another computer software company's software products which can provide similar or better software functions to replace its traditional software products easily. So, the training and learning development is one important factor to influence the computer software company whether its software sale number can be increased or decreased easily. It depends on the knowledge level of its computer software programmers. So, the software designing knowledge is every software programmer individual tangible asset to influence the computer software company's any kinds of software product sale number. It assumes that the software company can increase software sale number easily if it own many number of high software program designing skillful software programmers. Otherwise, if it own less number of high software program designing skillful software programmers. it can not increase software sale number easily, even it will decrease software products sale number.

Hence, it explains why some organizations need have skill satisfaction, such as computer software design organization case example, for HR to have a major role in software program designing organizational business strategy, it needs to have the kind of right software program designing skills to its different kinds of software program trainees. Highly correlated with HR's overall role in strategy are business partner skills, such as software program designing skills. Included in the scale are businss understanding, software designing strategic planning, how software organizational department's organization design and cross-functional experience of different kinds of software designing skills, e.g. who can be the kind of software designing trainer. it is harding surprising that these different kinds of software desinging skills are so strongl related to one computer software program desinging organizational HR's role in strategy. They are all critical and capability to engage in any computer software product sale organization's business decisions and to deliver organizational -level to different kinds of software programming products design method in one software product sale organization. It is consistent with the point that, to be a strategic partner to the software designing organization, such as the computer software trainers. HR needs to understand the computer software business, e.g. how to select the most excellent software designing trainers to teach the different kinds of software designing knowledge to their diffeent kinds of software designing trainees to learn in order to improve o upgrade their software program designing skills effectively.

In conclusion, it explains that every organization of strategic focus is different . It depends on whether what kinds of product it sells or what kinds of service it serves. Such as computer software product sale organization, it's strategic focus is how to design the different kinds of unique software products to satisfy software product , such as company software or individual software users' needs. Hence, training and learning department is one important department to influence its software product sale number. It must need excellent software trainers to teach their software trainee individual software designing knowledge in order to improve every one software designing skills in order to cope further software product buyers' needs, when it chooses th right training and learning strategic plan to train its software designing skills. Then, they can have more confidence to design any kinds of good quality of software products to sell in global software product market successfully, e.g. the software sale company can have new kinds of software products to promote to sell every three month. Hence, it seems that right strategic focus will influence right HR strategic plan to be implement to improve employee performance or better quality of software productive result. It explains that learning and training department is needed to computer software sale industry.

- Effective training on employee performanc

An effective training can maximize the job performance. Every organization' responsibility to enhance the job performance of the employees and certainly implementation of training and development is one of the major steps that most companies need to achieve this. Organizations need to utilize human resources effectively. Training of human resources needs to fit into the organization's structure as this it will make the organizations achieve their goals and objectives.

For telecommunication industry case example, how to carry on one effective training to raise employee efficiency. It includes these questions:

What training programs exist on the telecommunications sector? What are the training objectives what methods are used and do these methods meet the training objectives? How does training affect employee performance? Why does telecommunication industry employees need training is better? Training is a type of activity which is planned a systematic and it results in enhanced level of skill, knowledge, and competency that are necessary to perform work effectively.

In telecommunication organization, staffing needs to ensure that the right people are available at the right time in the right place. Thus involves identifying the nature of the job and implementing a recruitment and selection process to ensure a correct match within the organization. Training and development are often used to choose the gap between current performance and expected future performance.

How does training and development provide performance feedback, identifying individual strengths and weaknesses, recognizing individual performance, assisting in goals identification, evaluating goal achievement identifying individual training needs, determining organizational training needs, improving communication and allowing employees to discuss concerns.

There are a number of alternative source of appraisal includes to train telecommunication staffs, manager, supervisor appraisal is done by am employee's manager one level higher, self appraisal performance by the employee prior to the performance interview,

Reference

Ong Teong, W. (2010), Results management effective people management to acheve excellent results: Singapore, John Wiley & Sons (Asia) pte. ltd. pp.1-8.

● How human resource brings
benefits to organizations

Why do some organizations need human resource department(HRD)? Why do some organizations also need human resource strategy? What will occur if the organization has none human resource department? I shall attempt to explain as below:

Torraco, R.J. & Swanson, R.A. (1995) indicated that the role of HRD in organization strategic planning. Two factors have influenced HRD toward a more active role in the formulation of busines strategy. They include the centrality of information -technology to business success, and the sustainable competitive advantage offered by workforce expertise. These two factors work together in such a way that the competitive advantages they offer are nearly impossible to achieve without developing and maintaining a highly competent workforce.

What will be human resource department's positive influence to bring to organization's benefits? I assume that HRD is a more influential role at the point of strategy formulation and is becoming on of the key determinants of business strategy. Due to this rapidly changing business environment fator, it requires a dynamic strategy planning process and flexible use of resources . So, I assume that HRD is a formative role in both the strategic planning process and in developing innovative , competent human resources in large size organization.

In fact, human resource department can bring various benefits to large size organizations. Some benefits may be calculated , e.g. raising productive bumber, reducing employee turnover number, but other some benefits may only be feeling, e.g. improving employee engagement performance, building positive employee work attitude, building employee loyalty and organizational warming culture. So, if one large organization has one effective HR department, it can help the organization to achieve above these any one of aims easily.

Moreover, every human resource department ought have HR management strategy, it includes these elements: planning HR needs, staffing organizations based on HR needs, compensating and motivating employees, appraising employee behaviors, enhancing potential e.g. training and development, maintaining effective work relationships and work environment. Meeting current needs to every department staff, e.g. what are the application to the position's minimum requirement, whether the applicants need to raise skill level, knowledge, expertise, education level to apply the position. Forecasting when the department will have staff number shortage challenge ot excessive staffs number, it needs to plan when to need to reduce the staff number to some positions in the department before the deparment feels that it does not need extra employees in short time. Succession HR planning to ensure year organization can provide skillful training and learning knowledge to avoid talent employees and organizational knowledg lost. increasing maximum utilization of individuals to achieve organizational objectives, supervising employees to work efficiently and effectively in all levels.

Hence, HR department role is advisor. It needs to provide advice and services in the following areas. On an ongoing basis: maintenance of HR records, recuitment, selection, orientation, training and development, compensation and benefits , administration, employee counselling and labour relations. All HRM functions are interrelated as well as each function affects other areas. The functions include how to manage every employee's performance, it is one goal-oriented process directed toward ensuring organizational processes are in place to maximize productivity of mployees, teams as well as how to achieve formal system of performance as team task performance, how to achieve compensation to all rewards that individuals receive as a result of their employment.

Compensation can influence direct financial compensations, e.g. wages, salaries, bonuses and commission , indirect financial compensation (benefits), e.g. vacations, sick leave, holidays, and medical insurance, non-financial compensation , e.g. satisfaction that person receives from job itself or from psychological and/or physical environment in which person works. Employers also need to concern safety and health to its employees, such as protecting employees from injuries caused by work-related accident and freedom from illness and their general physical and mental well being: human resource activity is often referred to as industrial relations, because business is required by law to recognize a union and bargain with it in good faith if the firm's employees want the union to represent them, e.g. one airline firm's front line service employees plan to strike on job, due to they feel their salaries are below than market salary level. So, they will find union to represent them to complain the airline, e.g. stopping on continue to work in unlimited period. They will wait till to the airline management can meet them to discuss their unfair salary issue. Then, the airline needs have one HR compensation represent to be arranged on what day and time to plan how to meet them to solve their complaints. Hence, the airline labour relation represent needs have good negotiation skill to persuade them to continue to work in the shortest time in order to avoid airline travellers' dissatisfaction, due to planes are delayed to fly. So, HR department needs have good negotiation function to solve labour related issues nowadays.

However, human resource department's function , instead of selection, recuitment, reward, training, performance evaluation etc. functions. The benefits arrangement function is also very important to influence employee individual engagement to bring positive attitude to work in the organization. I shall indicate global public service (government)'s police force organization case for example to explain why whose human resource department needs to consider policemen benefits issues. Because if the country's public service police force organization can provide excellent benefits to encourage them to do catching thiefs activities hardly. Then, I believe that the country's crime rate to itself country will be fallen down , even to the miniumal level , zero crime occurrence. Then, it will influence the country's critizen will live in safe environment and many different countries travellers will choose to go to the safe country to travel in preference when they feel the country's crime rate is low, so the crime chance will be less to occur to the traveller himself/herself. When he/she is staying in the country's journey time.

I shall indicate Hong Kong (HK) public service police force organization example, its HR department is considering policeman individual welfare issue. It insource one welfare department to deal all policeman individual welfare needs. So, HK policemen individual welfare can include: insurance, free holiday living vacation appartment, subsidiary of travelling air ticket price allowance, HR policeman individual adult son or daughter whose overseas education subsidiary allowance, low market rate of rent private living quarters, low interest private loan , low interest education loan etc. different kinds of benefits. So, HK pubic service police force organization whose HR function is considering policeman individual welfare need. It aims to encourage every one has more engagement to catch any thiefs to achieve zero crime final result aim as well as it hope to let travellers feel safe to choose to travel to HK , this small city as well as it hopes HK citizen can feel safe to live HK to reduce emmigrant to overseas number. It seems that HK government's police force organization's welfare issue will be HR main function. It will follow different HK policeman individual beneficial nees to arrange the most satisfactory beneficial arrangement to provide their needs. So, it also seems HK policemen will consider whether HK police force employer can provide what kinds of benefits to persuade themselves to select to join to HK government police force organization to work. Hence, how to arrange different kinds of benefits to satisfy HK policemens' needs. It will be HK police force's main part of function for HK police force organization. When this organization has good benefits to satisfy HK policemens' extra need , instead of attractive salary and promotion rank chance.

Financial and non-financial benefits will be global police force organizations which need to consider matter if they hope their country policemen can have more engagement to do catching thiefs activities in order to achieve zero crime occurence final aim. Moreover, every private or public organizations' benefit policy can influence the organization's employees performance either improve or not improve. Because nowadays employee will consider whether the organization can give provide what kinds of benefits to encourage them to stay to the organization to work longer time. If the organization can provide attractive benefits to let its employees to feel financial and non-financial reasonable reward, instead of basic salary /wage reward. Then, reasonable benefits can enourage their working performance to be improved. So, any organizations' HR department ought consider whether whose organization's employees have any benefits need in order to reduce employees turnover number and imprve working performance and efficient working productivities. So, how to choose the suitable benefits arrangement issues , it will be future HR department's one part of important function to any private or public service organizations.

Finally, the another consideration is how to achieve HR planning. How it will provide the managerial function of an organization, such as it ensures adequate supply of human resource,, it ensures proper quality of human resource, it ensures effective utilization of human resource. However, human resource planning must incorporate the HR needs in the organizational goals, HR planning must be directed towards clear and well defined objectives. HR plan must ensure that it has the right number of people and the right kind of people at the right time doing work for which they are economically most euitable, HR planning should concern the principle of periodical reconsideration of new developments and extending the plan to cover the changes during the given long period. So, HR planning will given the organization to estimate and project the supply and demand for different categories of personnel in the organization for the years to come. For example, HRP can help the government to allocate its resources to the various sectors, e.g. agriculture, industry etc. depending upon the priority accorded to the particular sector. It can help industry sector to estimate the more accurate employee demand number and the labour market employee supply number in order to avoid employee shortage challenge or excessive employee number to the organization's different departments.

HR planning perios can include activities planning, daily and weekly (short term) e.g. the department supervisor writes specific actions, responsibilities, cost time schedule and organizational profitability , day-to-day and week -to-week plans and work schedule decentralized throughout the firm. The intermediate range planning (3-5 years) , e.g. deployment of resources, acquisitions, divestments and internal development of product line need for employee number increasing or decreasing arrangement. The strategic planning (5 to more years) long term, it is corporate philosophy value system and policies, goals and objectives, key success factors, product market scope, competitive allocation of resources, analysis of issues raised by external factors, employment demand and manpower supply analysis, forecasting total staffing level, number of managers and personal forecasting changes in managers and key personnel, activities , e.g. planning change whose current positions to seek another firm's positions or planning to promotion for the employee's career planning.

Consequently, HR department function will need to predict every employee individual activities and how to influence its organizational development, e.g. predicting the employee plans when to find nother employer to replace current employer, predicting when the employee hopes to earn promotion chance during he/she feels bored to do current job duties, predicting when the employee will feel his/her basic salary /wage is not reasonable and he/she needs extra welfares to be provides to satisfy his/her award needs. Hence, future HR department ought not consider how to improve group or team work performance to excite whole members' working performance. It ought serve it organizational employee individual's award needs, it seems to be one social worker role to consider whether what kinds of salary and benefits need to every employee individual who is actual hoping in order to avoide the employee turnover number increasing to bring training expenditure to need to be increased to train any new employees who replace the leaving employees. So, HR 's main function ought need to achieve to reduce the aim of employee turnover number to be increased for any organization in long term. An effective HR department which ought persuade any old employees to choose to stay to himself/herself organization to work for long term. This is HR department's one important strategic aim for any organizations nowadays because the resigning employees will attribute whose skills to another new firm when he/she chooses to leave his/her organization. Then, it means that the firm help the another competitor to raise its competitive effort from its training's any resigning employees. It will bring negative influence to replace its market position. So, how to persuade old employees to stay to itself's company to work for long term issue, it will be value to every firm's HR department to need to spend to research to solve their leaving reasons because every old employees will be any organization's assets.

reference

Torraco, R.J. & Swanson, R.A. (1995). The strategic roles of human resource development, HR planning, 18(4), pp.10-21.

CHAPTER NINE

Solving Human Resource International Organization Strategic Challenges

CHAPTER TEN

HUMAN RESOURCE ASSISTS ORGANIZATIONAL DEVELOPMENT

● Human resource assists change management strategic development

When on firm sets up one human resource department, whether it can assist itself organization to implement change management strategy more easily? What is change management mean? Change management is a critical part of any project that leads, manages, and enables people to accept new processes, technologies, systems, structures and values.

It is the activities that helps staffs to adapt good change management from present way of working to the desired way of working. So, change management is the continuous process of operation an organization with its marketplace in order to achieve more responsively and effectively than competitors.

In fact, any organization's change, it must strat with a vision. Anyway its changing need is from external environment factors influence, e.g. economic, social or technological or internal factors, e.g. policy, systems or structure , creating a vision wil clarify the direction for the change. In addition, the vision will assist in motivating those that are impacted to take action in the right direction. So it ensures that vision can assist change management more easily. However, whether human resource department strategy can follow the organization's vision to assist change management to implement more easily, when the organization feels need to change.

In fact, a strategy(HR) will ensure the vision is achieved more easily when the organization needs to change, it can provide direction for achieving the vision when its organization needs to change. Without a strategic plan and vision, the change effort will not be successful easily. Hence, when the organization decides to change, it also neds to change HR strategy, e.g. how to match the best employee to change his/her old position to do the right new position from company's internal staffs choices when it needs to change , how to redesign reard o compensate new staffs when they replace the old staffs to do the the old staffs' positions. It seems that HR strategy will need to change, when the organization needs to change its internal organizational structure.

However, the HR department needs to implement how to change some issues related to human resource matters, such as solving these HR problem when the organization needs to change, e.g. employee resistance, solving different communication breakdown, insufficient time devoted to training, reducing staff turnover during the organizational changing period, reduced costs exceeded budget. The change obstacles of employee resistance include solving the staffs relationship with the different department leaders' team to satisfy employee concerns on s personal acceptable level, asking for their feedback and responding to their concerns honestly and openly. The communication breakdown obstacles include communicating key information to employees on an on-going and consistent basis. Staff turnover obstacles include engaging the leader's team by involving them in the initiative, coaching, mentor and enriching their new roles.

Thus, HRD needs to particular the organizational change tasks, such as needs to know what the changes, their impact, rationale and benefits are, it needs to explain them to anyone to believe the chane in worthwhile, how th change is impacting the old staff individual existing workload, or it needs to communicate the need for change to explain the first steps, how the changing position staffs need to be supported and when they have achieved quick to gain benefits to themselves, it needs to explain how the changes impact the same group, what changes will happen and when, explaining the change leaders what know their responsibilities and the commitment expectations to their team memebers, describing what change has successfully occurred in these groups in the past, explaining how and why these changing staff can learn from what work did or did not well.

Hence, in the whole changing steps, HRD needs to participate every team through each stage of the change effort. The step one, it needs to assist organization to change urgent message to let staffs to know. The step two, it needs to buid a guiding team to help departmental staffs to adapt to changing tasks more easily. The step three, it needs to choose the right vision to give right direction to let organizational change method is implemented in a correct way. The step four, ot needs to commicate every for one-by-one to do empower action clearly, the need of help of changing staffs to create short -term wins in every changing process. Moreover, the HRD needs to consider thee matters do not work, such as focusing on building a rational business case, getting top management, approval, and ignoring all feeling, that are blocking change, ignoring a lack of urgency and immediately to create a vision and strategy. The HRD can not misunderstand the difficulty of driving people from their comfort zones. Hence, it needs have enough staffs number to already to replace the low skillful of employees when they can not adapt change to do the new tasks. Then, they will need have highly attractive people to be chosen to replace them to do the new changing of natural characteristic task to satisfy different department's needs after organization had changed its internal structure. Thus, HRD has responsibility to arrange enough staffs number and explains what the new changing tasks to let the changing task need of employees to know whether they ought how to do in order to adapt to do new changing of tasks more easily. Hence, it seems that HRD can assist organizatonal development when it decides to implement changing strategy in the organizational restructure changing period.

- HRD (human resource deapartment) assists training management strategic development

Does HRD assist training strategic arrangement more easily? When one large organization needs to spend too much expenditure for training and development. If it had not set up one human resource department to control its cost spending, it will be possible to implement poor trainings to cause failed training. Hence, if one HRD could help every different knids of training course to focus on issues, such as training methods, selecting the most right trainer to teach different training courses, program design and following trainee characteristics to choose the most right training courses to let them to learn. Then, it will be more easier to implement every training chouse to let trainees to learn successfully.

In fact, when one organization has none one effective Human resource department, it will bring high change of training failure. So, it seems that training failure has relationship with poor HRD, include: unskilled practitioner provides invalid training , skilled practitioner provides invalid training or valid training but learning does not transfer of valid training, learning transfer , but hierarchical level, organizational (dominant) is too much limited to grow up its human resource department to develop, lacking effective characteristics of human resource development, e.g. poor performance appraise standards, restricted standardized training.

All of these above issues will have relationship to HRD. HRD includes psychology, sociology, managment and adult education. This is not a comprehensive review of related to training effectiveness, HRD and organizatonal culture, but is intended to be representatives. HRD needs to know there is no single measure of training success, such as productivity or job satisfaction. There are numerous qualitative and quantitative evaluation, approaches useful in determining training effectiveness.

However, successful training depends on the benefits of various groups including: organizational leaders, supervisors, trainees, HRD managers and training facilitators. So, organizations need have one good HRD plan (human resource development) plan in order to train every training teachers to provide effective training courses to let every trainee to learn in order to apply to work to raise efficiency or improve performance successfully. So, HRD is important to influence every training whether it is successful or failure training course.

Thus, any large organization needs have one effective HRD strategy in order to provide enough number of excellent training teachers (trainers) to assist its different departments to provide useful training courses to let every trainee to learn. Every trainer individual knowledge, skill, working experience will help his/her organization to train the new employment staff to learn their knowledge, skill effectively. So,, it seems that one effective HR department can assist its organization to develop HR (trainers) to be excellent training teachers to teach their traineers (new employment staffs) to absord their knowledge, skill to prepare to do their new position more to avoid none training cost waste successfully.

- HRD (human resource department) assists
diversity in the workplace to be benefits

Nowadays, globalization requires more interaction among people from diverse background. So, large organizations will need to consider when they have need to develop overseas markets. Their offices will have different countries' staffs to cooperate to work together. For this reason, profit and non-profit organizations need to become more diversified to remain competition. Maximizing and capitalizing on workplace diversity is an important issue for management. It brings this question: Can human resource department assist the organization's diversity development in order to let continue people to cooperate to work in order to raise performance or productivity or efficieny easily. For example, if the organization's HRD is effective, the interviewers can ensure to help their organizations to select whether what countriess' applicant whom is the most right applicant to do the departmental tasks, one China company's finance department needs one applicant who familizes US accounting/finance policy knowledge and owns US related finance and accountinr working experience to do this fiance manager position. Then, the China fiem needs to decide whether it ought to select the foreign US country's domestic applicant who owns many years of finance and accounting working experience and US accounting/finance university subject knowledge to do this finance manager position or select itself country's China domestic applicant who owns US finance/accounting related working experience and familizes US accounting/finance subjects knowledge. Although, if the China company selected the local applicant who owns finance/accounting knowledge and US company finance/accounting related working experience to do this finance manager positin. The advantages are that the finance manager and whose finance team staffs who can speak fluent chinese language. So, the finance manager and his/her finance department staffs can communicate to bring easier cooperation. But, it does not guarantee that he/she must lead or supervise his/her finance deparment staffs to raise peformance or efficiency daily. Otherwise, if the China firm select one foreign US applicant to do this finance manager position. Although, this US foreign finance manager can not speak fluent Chinese languare and he/she can only speaks American language. It is possible that the finance department staffs who all are Chinese. They can not understand English language easier. It is possible to bring communication difficult problem between the US foreign finance manager and his/her finance department staffs. But, the US foreign finance manager who has competitive effort is that his/her local US finance/accounting related working experience and university graduation of finance/accounting subject knowledge is better to compare to all China applicants whose own similar accounting/finance knowlege and related working experience in China. It seems that the foreign US finance manager applicant can perform more excellent to compare all China domestic finance manager applicants. If the finance manager's duty needs to familiarize US acocunting/finance policy to calculate tax and profit for US government tax department , due to this firm needs to sell products to US market often. It is possible that the foreign US finance manager applicant can lead or supervise whose finance department staffs to raise efficiency to work more easily, due to his/her familiar US accounting/finance policy and working experience is useful more than the China local applicants who owns more China accounting/finance knowledge and China accounting/finance related working experience.

Due to this finance manager position needs the applicant must own many years US firm accounting/finance working years and US education is prefer. Hence, HRD needs to consider diversity of workplace problem when it decides to employ one US foreign applicant to do this finance manager position to replace China local applicant to supervise or lead all Chinese staffs to work in finance department. So, knowing how to supervise finance staffs to cooperate to work efficiently and raise performance which will be the applicant's strength to do this position to the US applicant. However, the US foreign finance manager' s language and culture , education level, related finance and accounting working experience must be different to all Chinese finance staffs. Hence, workplace diversity issue will be this organization's HRD which needs to concern hoe to let different Chinese finance staffs and the American finance manager to easier adapt to work together in this company's finance department.

The best method is that this company's HRD needs to employ both Chinese and American people who can cooperate to work in human resource department together. The advantage is that when this company's HRD has these two countries' people to work, they can apply themselve countries' HR working experience and HR management knowledge to choose the most right applicants to do the positions, e.g. the finance deparment needs one finance manager, the US HRD manager can give better recommendation to know how to choose the best US finance manager.

Hence, in any diversity organizations, supervisors and managers need recognize the ways in which the workplace is changing. Managing diversity is significant organizational challenge. So, the diversity organizations' HRD needs to select the applicants who own more different countries' working experience and managerial skills in order to adapt to accommodate a multicultural working environment. The department manager applicants need have different countries effectively manage diverse workforces. It provides a general definition for workforce diversity, discusses the benefits and challenges of managing diverse workplace, and presents effective strateges for managing diverse workforce. Moreover, the diverse organization's HRD needs have effective performance evaluation strategy to review manager individual management practices and develop new and creative approaches to managing people. They aims to bring positive changes will increase work performance and customers service to let their organization can develop in diverse organizational working environment.

Why does diversity in the workplace need to occur to satisfy future some organizations' needs? Significant changes in the workplace have occurred , due to downsizing and outsourcing, which has greatly affected the organization's human resource management needs to be changed also. For example, globalization and new technologies have changed workplace practices, and there has been a trend toward longer working hours. Generaly speaking, organizational restructuring usually results, in fewer people doing more work. So, some organizations' HRD needs to select the efficient workers to continue to serve their departments.

When they need to discuss the non-efficient or below productive workers, again recruiting the new efficient working applicants to replace them. It is future organizational restructuring tend. So, any organization's HRD needs to concern how to devise to keep the most efficient workers to continue to serve for their organizational departments and how to select the most efficient applicants to do the jobs after the organization restructures.

What benefits of diversity in the workplace are bought to the diverse organizations? Diversity is beneficial to both employees and employers. Although, employees are interdependent in the workplace, respecting individual differences can increase productivity. Diversity in the workplace can reduce lawsuits and increase marketing opportunities, e.g. foreign sale market development, recruitment of the most right overseas applicants to do the jobs which need overseas educational learning knowledge and overseas working experiene, creating and building good business image to overseas market. When flexibility and creativity are keys to competitiveness, diversity is critical for a organization's sussess. Also, the consequences of loss of time and money should avoid.

Hence, future department managers need to own managing a diverse work population working experience when their organizations are international. Training department also needs to provide training courses to train new employing managers to learn how to deal more simply acknowledging differences in people. It involves learn how to teach every team's staffs to accept recognizing the value of differences, learn how to deal combating discrimination, and learn how to make reasonable decision to select whom can be the right staff to be promote as well as learn how to deal complaints an dlegal action against the organization. Due to different countries people work together to non necessary cause argument.

However, HRD and department managers need to know negative attitudes and behaviors can be barrier to organizational diversity because they can harm working relationships and damage morale and work productivity. Negative attitudes and behaviors in the workplace include: prejudice, discrimination, which should never be needed by management for hiring and termination practices, it can lead to raise organizational cost in long term , because the organization will have many overseas staffs choose to resign, if they felt discrimination is serious. Then these organizations will have lost any talent overseas staffs , due to their designation, any team efficiency will reduce, even performance will be poor when any team lacks talent overseas or different countries staffs and itself local staffs to work together. Hence, management level to staffs, e.g. supervisors, managers need to be trained to learn how to avoid to bring negative attitudes and behaviors to let overseas foreign countries staffs to feel unhappu to work together.

Training needs to be provides to train managers to be effective and are aware that certain skills are necessary for creating a successful , diverse workforce . For example, managers must understand discrimination and its consequences. Also, managers must recognize their own cultural biases and prejudices. Diversity is not about differences among groups, but rather about differences among individuals. Each individual is unique and does not repesent or speak for a particular group. Even, managers also need be willing to change organization of necessary. HRD also needs to provide training to let organization leaders , e.g. The lacking overseas working experience of CEO needs to learn how to manage diversity in the workplace to be successful in the future. So, training needs concentrate on teaching high, middle and low management level staffs' managerial skill how to corporate with different countries' staffs or lead or supervise them to work efficiently, happily, unfortuately. It is not easy to train these management skill to them. It mainly depends on the manager's ability to understand what is best for the organization based on teamwork and the dynamic of the workplace.

In fact, managing diversity is a process for creating a work environment that everyone. When creating a successful diverse workplace, an effective manager should focus on personal awareness. Both managers and team members need to be aware of their personal biases. These organizations need to develop , implement and maintain ongoing training because a one day session of traing won't change people's behavior. Managers need to concern these issues in diversity working environment: social gatherings and business neetings,where every member must listen adn have the chance to speak, are good ways to create happy working environment, managers need implement policies, such as mentoring programs to provide different countries staffs access to information and opportunities.

In conclusion, HRD needs to concern how to let a diverse workforce environment to implement effectively, how to let diverse work teams bring high value to organizations, how to let individual difference to bring benefit the workplace by creating a competitive effort and increasing work productivity, how to lead or train diversity management benefits every team by creating a fair and safe workplace environment where everyone has access to opportunities and challenges. Finally, HRD will need to train management leve staffs, e.g. supervisor, manager, CEO in a diverse workforce, it should be used to to educate every team members about diversity and its issues, including organization policies and regulations. Most workplaces are made up of diverse cultures, so organizations need to learn how to adapt to be successful. This is important successful factor to a diverse organization.

- Effective human resource department characteristics

What is the strengths and weaknesses between owning human resource organization and lacking human resource organization? How to achieve more effective human resource department development on organizational raising productivity? In fact, effective human resource development can enhance productivity in order to reduce poor performance in organization. For example: enhancing the efficiency of human resource training to train many excellent performance staffs aim from the human resource training function. It brings this question: Whaat factors determine and identify to affect human resource development and organizational productivity and changing positive attitude of the senior management to raise their managerial efforts successfully?

Human resource development is the engagement of people to work in order to achieve sales growth and profitability. How to make sure that the effort of employers are appraised from time to time to find out how they contribute to the achievement of organizational goals, and also raising educational qualifications for recruitment, selection, promotion and placement of workers more effective.

I assume that effective human resource management enables employees to contribute effectively and productivity to overall company direction and accomplishment of the organization's foals and objectives. If every human resource related tasks or functions , such as recruitment, selection, orientation, training, appraisal, motivation functions can achieve perfect aims in the shorten time efficiently, then the organization will have implement one effective human resource department.

This effectice HR related functions will ensure its stable continuity and achievement to the organization. However, I believe personal element is the main factor to raise organization's effectiveness to compare other kinds of factors, e.g. good machine facilities , good working environment, good employee morale and organizational policy etc. factors. If the organization has good qualities of personnel element. Consequently, the organization should prioritize the development of the human element to maximize talents, skills and ability which will automatically reflects on the company's profit. So, it seems that company's profit raising up or falling down , it has relationship to good or bad personnel element. One firm seems to be an auto-mental machine factory, it needs to employ some people , through a conventional plant with similar capacity might require more people. So, the company (factory) needs good personnel element for proper HR planning to employ the suitable workers to do the right job positions, it is known as a "manpower planning".

Hence, training is one important function to some organizations, when the organization needs to train lacking technicians or raise to improve their modern skills of improve upon their talents and educational qualifications when it selects to employe these low skillful employees to do its any departments' high technical skillful jobs when the organization needs to change. Thus, the technical workers need to be equip themselves skills which will boost quality product and profit making of their organization.

If focuses on raising raising productivity through improved quality, efficiency , cost reduction, and enabling customers concentrate on their core business activities, such as one vehicle manufacture factory needs have one effective training deparment to train whose vehicle manufacturing workers to learn how to apply artificial intelligence (AI) technological robots to manufacture good quality vehicles number to supply to overseas markets to sell in short time efficiently. Thus, the vehicle factory focuses on raising vehicle number productivity through improved artificial intelligence and skillful workers' skills to achieve raising vehicle quality in efficient way, and reducing employee number and salary cost and satisfying vehicle customers' different kinds of new vehicle design driving needs from artificial intelligent technological manufacturing.

However, some business is full of uncertainty and understanding of labour contribution or human resources development to training / raising management level staffs' managerial skills of boosting organizational productivity and as well as its profitability . I believe raising managerical skills to managers, which will assist to whom to raise effective productivity or efficiency to different departments. Why can training raise or improve managerial skills to managers ? The reasons are that the challenges of lack of skilled labour, heavy competition among firms, technological problem, low productivity and then rate of poor performance and poor product implementation when placing a serious limitation on product expansion and increase increase in productivity. If the organizatin has no enough high managerial skillful level of managers to know why and how to manage their team members to work efficiently in the organizational structural high technological changing working environment. Then, the poor skillful employees won't adapt to work in high technological changing working environment, such as artificial intelligence manaufacturing working environment. Then, it will be reduce productivities inefficiently, due to lacking high level owning managerial skillful of managers to supervise or lead them to work in one high managerial efficient way.

Hence, future HR development to train or raise managerial skills to different department managers. it seems to need have one essential HR training policy to any organizations if they hope to innovate to rsise productivity and efficiency successfully. I assume that the effective human resource development can enhance productivity in order to avoid poor performance as well as efficiency of human resource training to managers can result in organizational growth.

An effective HRM involve maintaining and improving all aspects of a company's practices. Hence, HR manager must devise the most efficient and cost -effective means of hiring, e.g. advertising and recruit for vacant positions. HR management team must devise and implement the selection procedures to choose the mot suitable candidates establish paying welfare and salary policy efficiently.

What factors can influence employee performance appraisal system? Has it relationship between good employee performance appraisal system and raising productivity or improving efficiency? One effective employee performance appraisal system can let human resource department to raise service efficiency to assist the organization to raise whole human resource long term development (human planning). An effective performance appraisal system can meet targets to acceptable quality standards and benchmarks as determined in each category of human resource service delivery. One effective employee performance appraisal system should be supported by training of staff, particularly those with managerial and supervisory responsibility , and the process should be regarded as interactive for multural agreement between supervisors and appraisers.

In fact, if one organization has one effective employee performance appraisal system, it can encourage employees to work hard, raise efficiency and productive performance more easily. It is one good tool for human resource management and performance improvement. The process of performance management involves the identification of common goals between the appraiser and the appraisee. It must relate to the overall organizational goals. To test each employee performance, such as if a process is conducted effectively. It will increase productivity and quality of output when the department(S) staffs who had ever participated the process. Hence , the performance appraisals , accuracy and fairness in measuring employee performance is very important. Performance management is a control measure used to determine which work tasks with a view of taking corrective action. It is also used to reflect on past performance as the organization plans ahead. So, provision of feedback on the required corrective action to let every employee to know whether why and how he/she has done error in order to let he/she to revise whose error is critical in the process. For the appraisals to be effective, the top management must be supportive in providing information, clear performance standards must be set, the appraisals must not be used for any other purpose apart from performance management and the evaluation must be free from any rating biases. However, comparing the employees' performance from the performance appraisal is important in making future improvement. The performance appraisals are supported to be conducted at least twice annually to be better than once annually. The annual performance appraisals also need to help in determining how every employee fits into the organizational development and efficiency in performing all the assigned tasks and responsibilities. Moreover, it also needs to help in determining the training needs of the employees in planning future job schedules.

Additionally, the kind of working environment that is needed to be created by the performance appraisals optimizes the employees' work performance. Then, departmental and individual objectives are needed to formulate which will be consistent with the organizational objectives. In fact, training is one method to raise employee performance. The raters should be trained on various aspects, like supervision skills, conflict resolution, coaching, setting performance standards, linking this system to pay, and how to provide employee feedback. The training will equip ratees with expertise and knowledge what they need in making decision in the course of the process.

What factors will influence employee performance appraisal system successfully? They include formal meetings factor, individual performance should need be discussed. The performance review may include the actual performance, the tasks that are completed and areas that need improvement. It aims to achieve " action inquiry" to let employee individual or every team has chance to enquire whether how to improve productive performance questions in order to earn more effective recommendations. The another factor is feedback, it is an important part of one effective employee performance appraisal systems. The feedback should be specific and timely and be against the predetermined performance expectations. So, every employee has right to know how who are progressing in performing the assigned tasks and to receive feedback. However, feedback should need to be provided on a continuous basis, e.g. daily, weekly or monthly more better than two weekly or half year period.

In conclusion, poor performance evaluation won't havve the desired effect. There should be a proper development of the appraisal to remove subjectivity and bias in the ratings. Because the appraiser's subjective bias will cause the inaccurate measurement to every staff individual actual performance to decide whether he/she ought need to be promoted or not. Hence, removing subjectivity and bias in the ratings of appraiser personal poor performance evaluation factor will be very important to achieve one effective employee performance appraisal plan to bring either positive efficient method.

- Effective training on employee performance

An effective training can maximize the job

performance. Every organization's respensibility to enhance the job performance of the employees and certainly implementation of training and development is one of the majoe steps that most companies need to achieve this organizations need to utilize human resourcee effectively. Traning of human resource needs to fit into the organization's structure as this it will make the organizations achieve their goals and objectives.

For telecommunication industry case example, how to carry on one effectively training into raise employee efficiency. It includes their questions: What training programs exist the telecommunications section? What are the training objectives? What methods are used and do these methods meet the training objectives? How does training affect employees performance? Why does telecommunication industry employees need better training? Training is a type of activity which is planned a systematic and it results in enhanced level of skill, knowledge, and competency that are necessary to performance work effectively.

In telecommunication organization, staffing needs to ensure that the right people are available at the right time in the right place. This involves identifying the nature of the job and implementing a recruitment and selection process to ensure a correct match within the organization. Training and development are often used to chose the gap between current performance and expected future performance. How does training and development provide performance feedback, identifying individua strengths/weaknesses, recognizing individual performance, assisting in goal identification, evaluating goal achievement, identifying individual training needs, determining organizational training needs, improving communication and allowing employees to discuss concerns?

There are a number of alternative sources of appraisal includes: Training telecommunication front line staffs, supervisors, managers appraisal are done by an employee's manager one level higher, self appraisal performance done by the employee prior to the performance interview, subordinate appraisal: appraisal of a supervisor is by an employee, which is more appropriate for developmental than for administrative purposes. Peer appraisal is by follow employees for use in an interview conducted by the employee's manager, team appraisal based on total quality management concepts, recognizing team accomplishment's rather than individual performance, customer appraisal that seeks evaluation from both external and internal customers.

Training is a planned and systematic modification of behavior through learning events, activities and programs which result in the participants achieving the levels of knowledge, skills, competencies and abilities to carry out their work effectively. The main purpose of training is a acquire and improve knowledge, skills and attitudes towards work related tasks. It is one of the most important potential motivators which can lead to both short-term and long-term benefits for individuals and organizations. It can raise high morale, employees who receive training have increased confidence and motivations, lower cost of production, training eliminates risks because trained personnel are able to make better and economic use of material and equipment thereby reducing and avoiding waste, lower turnover, training brings a sense of secutiry as the workplace, reduces labour turnover and absenteeism is avoided.

Change management, training helps to manage change by increasing the understanding and involvement of employees in the change process and also provides the skills and abilities needed to adjust to new situations, providing recognition, enhanced, responsibility and the possibility of increased pay and promotion, helping to improve the availability and quality of staff.

An effective training needs to focuse on workers' performance, improving certain: working practices, this focuses on improvement regardless of the performance problems and changing or renewing the organization situation, which may arise because of innovations or changes in strategy. When the organization feels training need, it needs to create , develop maintain and improve any systems relevant in contributing to the availability of people with required skills. Moreover, training programs should be designed to carter for the different needs.

Furthermore, HR , the training programme, content and the trainees' chosen depend on the objectives of the training programme. There are two different methods that organizations may choose from for training and developing skills of its employees. There are on-the-job training given to organizational employees then conducting their regular work at the same working venues and off-the -job training involves taking employees away from their usual work environments and therefore all concentration to the training. Examples of the on-job training include but are not limited to job rotations and transfer, coaching and/or mentoring.

On the other hand, off-the job training examples include conferences, role playing. Different organizations are motivated to take or different training methods for a number of reasons for example: depending on the organization's strategy, goals and resources available, depending on the needs identified at the time and the target groups to be trained which may include among others individual workers, groups, teams department or the whole organization.

Job rotation and transfers is as a way of developing employee skills within organization involves movements of employees from on official responsibility to another for example taking on higher rank position within the organization, and one branch of the organization to another. For transfers for example, it would involve movement of employees from one country to another. These rotations and transfers facilitate employees acquire knowledge of the different operations within the organization together with the differences existing in different countries, where the organization operates.

The knowledge is acquired by the selected employees for this method is beneficial to the organization as it may increase the competition advantage of the organization. In every training, trainees are provided with some information related the description of the roles, concerns objective, responsibilites, emotions.

In conclusion, effective training needs have these requirements, identifying and defining training needs, defining the learning required in terms if what skills and knowledge have to be learnt and what attitudes need to be changed, defining the objectives of the training, planning training programs to meet the needs and objectives combination for training technique and locations, deciding who provides the training, evaluating training amending and extending training as necessary.

- Designing effective pay for performance compensation system

One effective pay compensation system can give fair rewards to encourage employees hard to work, including front line employees and top level managers to individual , team and/or organizational achievement, short term or/and long term goals, efforts or outcomes when external constraints exist. Employees can be rewarded by one time cash bonus, increase to base pay or combination. So, effective pay reward system will improve performance evaluation process. For example, rewarding individuals who generate the greatest amount of output may be appropriate in some organizations that are very production-oriented.

It could be problematic in an organization whose work demands closed attention to how results are achieved particularly, in regard to matters , such as quality , safety or teamwork. A performance system can only be effective if employee is value the pay or recognition that the organization offers in return for high performance, understand what is required of them, believe that they can achieve the desired level of performance, and believe that the organization will actually recognize and reward that performance.

How to design fair reward measurement? For example, supervisors will need training in designing performance measures and providing performance feedback , a performance evaluation system that enables them to accurately distinguich among levels of performance, and guidelines for determining pay increases or performance bonuses. A fair pay reward system will have these characteristics: performance goals and measures are relevant, reasonable and usable, employees understand and participate in the performance evaluation process and performance is evaluated fairly.

However, an effective pay reward system can help employees to understand what is expected of them, to choose wisely among various courses of action, and to identify, seek and obtain the resources (such as training and equipment that they need to succeed). A pay for performance system can not have these desirable effects unless employees understand the organization's goals, their role in achieving these goals and how the pay system works.

How can be a pay for performance system? Outstanding performaners will receive the greatest reward , to acknowledge their supervisor contributions and to motivate them to continue high performance. Average performers will receive substantially smaller raises, which may encourage them to work harder to achieve larger raises in the future, poor performaners will receive no increase, which is intended to persuade them to improve their performance or leave.

How to implement an affective selection? Effective selection process which needs assessment to determine the current and future human resource requirements of the organization. If the activity is to be effective, the human resource requirements for each job category and functional division/unit of the organization must be assessed and a priority assigned, identification within and amends are be valued the employees, the awards are often to be given, how often the rewards are reviewed, the award is long or short term.

Legal framework for reward system, such as payment of wage, restriction on wages deduction, minimum wage, benefit, such as share options o housing benefits. Major benefits plans include: retirement benefit schemes, personal security , e.g. healthcare, dental , hospitalization, accident or life insurance, financial assistance, e.g. mortgage interest subsidies, rental subsidies, staff discount, education subsidies, personal needs, e.g. holidays and leave pay, child care , fitness and facilities, use of holiday house etc. employee shares purchase plan, company car, identification within and outside the organization of the resource pool and the likely competition for the knowledge and skills resident within it, job analysis and job evaluation to identify the individual aspects of each job and calculate its relative worth, assessment of qualifications profiles, drawn from job descriptions that identify responsibilities and required skills , abilities , knowledge and experience determination of the organizational ability to pay selection and benefit within a defined period, identification and determination of the actual process of restructure and selection to ensure equity and the equal opportunity. Hence, all of these will be on effective recruitment process factor to choose the most right applicants to do the positions method.

- ? How to Judge whether the training is effective?

Effective training can raise employee individual
performance and efficiency. Otherwise, inefficient training can increase cost, and waste time and trainer individual resource as well as it can bring negative reducing efficiency and poor performance and poor morale to employee individual negative emotion influence. Hence, organizations need to consider whether the training can bring positive influence to satisfy employee individual raising skills and knowledge level need to be applied to do those tasks. If the training seems that it is ineffective. I recommend that organization ought not to spend time, resource to implement the training.

Daniel G. (2015, pp.79) states that if a company hires correctly, workers will want to be super performers, and they can be managed through honest communication and common sense. Most companies focus too much on formal policies and at the small number of employees whose interests aren't fully applied with the firm's. Hence, the author believes that super performance employees do not need their organization's formal policies to manage them. They must communicate to their team supervisors honestly. Because they hope their employers believe their efforts to feel they ought increase salary to earn fair rewards due to they are superior performance employees. Hence, it means that whether the training is either effective or ineffective, it is not important to train the super performance staffs. If the ineffective training is provided to the superior performance staffs (trainees) to learn. It will bring negative influence to reduce their effort to do the tasks because they feel their employers do not believe they are super performance staffs. So, it is not important to train them, it means that what training must not need to be provided to train all these owning superior performance employees. The training is time waste, resource and money to teach them if their new hired workers can own good knowledge and skill to do their tasks.

So, the company ought not decide to implement training to teach them when they are recruited in beginning, due to it feel they are foolish, unskillful and lacking knowledge workers to do their tasks. It ought spend time to wait, e.g. spending three month or more time to wait in order to observe their behaviors when their efficiency and performance can improve to satisfy it's the least task requirement. Then it can make more accurate or right judgement to find whom will be the super performer worker(s), who do(does) not need to be trained.

In general, one company implement formal policies to aim to manage small number of employees more effective, due to it feels they are difficult communication employers. But, another feels it is not effective to improve their performance. Daniel, G. (2015, pp.79) explains that solution is that hire, reward and tolerate only fully formed adults. Tell the truth about performance. Make clear to managers that their top priority is building great teams. Leaders should create the company culture, and talent managers should think like innovative business people and mot fall into the traditional. human resource mindset.

Hence, raising rewards is not effective method to encourage workers to work hardly. Companies ought not only concentrate on raising reward to employees in order to feel it can excite their productivity and raising efficiency. It is very wrong decision, companies ought design any actual effective training courses to raise every team leader or department leader individual managerial skills or efforts and knowledge level in order to manage himself/herself team members to work in order to improve performance or raise efficiency more effectively.

Hence, any training trainee target and training course designing need must be chosen how to implement carefully in order to avoid to implement the wrong or ineffective training course to let the wrong training target trainees to learn, e.g. if the different team or department supervisor or leader individual skill and knowledge need is more important to be trained more useful than their staffs' needs. It means that the different department or team manager individual managerial skills is more needed to be raised or improved to achieve the raising efficiency or improving performance consequence or aim to compare to train every staff individual skill and knowledge level. Then, the organization ought concentrate on designing any useful managerial skill training courses in order to raise their managerial skill and knowledge to know how to achieve to manage themselves' department or team 's workers or staffs to do their tasks more efficient or more performance improvement effectively.

In conclusion, effective training implement is depended on whether the course's choice learning target trainees whom are right learning target trainees or not as well as how to design the training course's teaching contents whether it is actual useful or help in order to raise the trainee individual efficiency and improve performance effectively.

Reference

Daniel G (2015) . The definitive management ideas of the year from Harvard business review, HBR's 10 must reads . Boston , US, Harvard business school publishing, pp.79.

CHAPTER ELEVEN

HOW HUMAN RESOURCE DEVELOPMENT ASSISTS ORGANIZATIONS TO RAISE PRODUCTIVE EFFICIENCY

In any organizations, instead of their human resource department function includes: interview, selecting, training, peformance evaluation management, reward management etc. based human related responsibilities. Can human resource department assist any other departments to raise employee individual productivies and efficiencies? Although, it has only indirect relationship to productivity and efficiency issue. It does not represent that it can not assist any departments to attempt to raise employee individual productivity and efficiency. I shall indicate evidences to explain how it will possible occur.

How to impact human resource (HR)management on turnover productivity and corporate financial performance? I believe that HR development has an economically and statistically significant impact on both intermediate employee outcomes (turnover and productivity) and short and long term measures of corporate financial performance.

In fact, the impact of human resource management policies and practices on firm performance is an important topic in the fields of human resource management. The high performance work practices may include comprenhensive employee recruitment, selection procedures, incentive compensation and performance management system , and implementing employee engagement, training strategies, which can improve the knowledge, skills, and abilities of a firm's current and potential employees.

However, arguments made in related research are that a firm's current and potential human resources are important considerations in the development and execution of the firm's strategic plan. It brings this question: How and why organization's human resource development plan which can assist to raise employee individual productive efficiency. I shall assume that one organizational human resource policies, if it is effective, then it can bring properly contribution to provide a diect and economically significant contribution to the firm.

An organization's effective HR department development is needed to support by the development and vaidation of an instrument that reflects the system of high performance work practices adpted by the firm's employees. Then, if the organization has high performance work practices, it implies that its all employees had adopted its working environment to do every task efficiently. The reasons include as below points:

The first point, their employees must add value to the firm's production processes from effective training methods to achieve raising levels of individual performance successfully.

The second point, the skills to the firm seeks must be rare. So, the firm's employees can have rare skills to contribute to their organization to compare the other similar industry's organizations, their owning general ordinary skills of employees. So, rare skillful employees and effective training both methods which will be important factors to assist different departments to improve performance and raise productive efficiency more easily. Also, it implies that an effective Hr department will have above characteristics when the organization's human resource department owns above these competitive advantages. Then, achieving the raising productivity and efficiency aim will achieve more easily.

The third point, the human resource department needs to have long-term human capital development to invest to the firm's employees to continue to train them to improve their hard and soft both skills. Investments in human resource development, they are similar to organization's equipment or facilities investments. So, they both are such as to invest in the firm's specific human captial, which can further decrease the probability of such imitation by qualitatively differentiating between the firm's specific talent employees and the other same industry firms' employees .Thus, it means that the firm's employees' skills and efforts will be better to compare its same industry competitors' employees, if the firm has long-term human resource talent development strategy to its different departments' employees to prepare to raise heir skills and efforts level.

The final point, a firm's human resources must not be subject to replacement by technological development, e.g. artificial intelligence, computer, information technology, internet or other substitutes of they are to provide a source of competitive advantage. Although, when the organization can choose to apply technologies investment to replace all employees or many employees to do their tasks in order to manufacture any products. However, the labor saving technological method is not suitable to half-service industry. For example, a restaurant can use robots to replace waitors to deliver food to clients to eat. It is simple food delivery tasks. But it is not good to apply robots to replace cookers to do their cooking tasks, because robot cooker's cooking skill, it is difficult to imitate human cooker's cooking skill in order to make same or similar ,even better food taste to let restaurant clients to feel better food taste. For the restaurant's cashier task example, because casher;s calculation ability will be netter to compare (AI) 's calculation ability. Human cashier's calculation error chance will be lesser to compare robot cashier's calculation skills. So , if the restaurant's all cookers, waitors and cashiers whose tasks all are replaced by robots. It will bring under utilized consequence because robots can not perform above their maximum potential more easier than human employees in the restaurant's long term working hours every day, because the restaurants employ more than one staff to prepare to replace the staff when he/she feels tired to need rest. Otherwise, these all restaurant positions , it has only one robot to do its position in the restaurant. I believe that these three cashier and cooker and waitor robots will be used to the maximum of utilization , then they will be older and calculation, walking and cooking speed and effort will also be slow and poor when they are used long hours every day to serve clients in the restaurant.

Thus, when one service organization, it can not only concentrate on robots to replace human employees to do their positions' all tasks. It will perform worse than the service organizaion , it only uses robots to replace some employees to do some tasks and some positions still use human employees to do themselves tasks. Otherwise, one manufacturing organization, e.g. car manufacturing organization, it may apply robots to participate some part of human employees' manufacturing tasks in the car manufacturing process. It will help human empoyees to manufacturing can productivities and efficiencies more than the another car manufacturing firm only employs human workers to manufacture all cars in car manufacturing process every day. When the later car manufacturing neglects to apply robots to participate the whole car manufacturing process to assist human workers to manufacture cars. Then, the later only applying human workers' car manufacturing firm which will have worse productivities and inefficiencies to compare the prior car manufacturing firm to apply both robots and human workers to manufacture any kinds of cars in whole car manufacturing process. The reason is because human workers must feel tried when they need concentrate their nevous to manufacture many cars every day. If robots can participate their car manufacturing tasks to share work load to assist they to finish some more difficult or complex part of tasks, then they will feel less nervous and they reduce pressure to manufacture the complex part of car manufacturing process. Then, their efficiency and productive performance will be raised in possible.

● Can HRM practice influence employee individual skills through the HR development of a firm's human capitals in organization?

It will need long time to implement HR development in any organization, if the organization decides to implement long term HR development strategy, e.g. it can provide formal and informal training experiences, such as basic skills training, on-the-job experience, coaching, mentoring, and managemet development can further influence employee individual skills to be improved in other to achieve raising productive efficiency to every department.

Other raising productivity and efficient method is that employee psychological method. The HRM practices can attempt to encourage employees themselves motivates to work both harder and smarter. So, when some employees have higher skills, they can do tasks more better , but these igher skillful employees limit their effort to work in lazy. So, their productive efficiency can not achieve the best performance. The question is concerned how to persuade or encourage them to motivate and perform work hard? The solution may be performance appraisals that assess individual or work group performance, linking these appraisals to incentive compensation systems, the use of internal promotion systems that can focus on employee merit, e.g. the performance evaluation may have three levels:excellent performance, good performance and poor performance three levels. Thus, the oftenhigh performance employees can earn more reward to compensate their efforts or promote them to higher positions in

short time in order to persuade how they perform their tasks to improve their productivities and efficiencies in short time.
The another raising productive efficient method is to change organizational culture to be better. It seems that organizational culture can influence turnove. I shall assume that it has relationship between productivity and organizational culture. For example, if the organization's culture or policy is not one punishment method. Then, it can enourage the lazy workers to apply many leaving pay holidays and the lazy workers will be encouraged to absence and the absenteeism number will increase. It needs to change its traditional organizational culture in order to threaten the lazy employees need to hard to work. When the firm changes punishment method to treat these often absent employees, then these lazy workers number will be possible to reduce, due to they do not want be punished. When the organization has punishment method and disciplinary actions to treat the employees who have higher absenteeism, due to they feel afraid to be punished. Thus, the positive consequencey may be increasingly product quality and direct labor efficiency, lower absenteeism, and labor high teams increased productivity.
In conclusion, it seems that when one organization can achieve to implement one long term human resource management development strategy to its any departmental employees, it have more chance to bring long term raising productivities and efficiencies and improving employee individual behavioral performance consequence.

● Human resource raising productive
efficient factors

Why some organizations' productive efficiency can be improved? Otherwise, why some organizations' productive efficiency can not be improved? Does it has relationship between the organization's efficiency and effective human resource (HR) strategy? I shall indicated some cases to explain why it is possible that an ineffective HR department strategy which will influence inefficiency and low productive performance to the organization in long term.
How to achieve efficienct organizational behavior, it depends on many factors. However, effective training can raise employee individual efficiency, due to the effective training can raise the employee individual confidence to do whose task.

1.0 Effective training preparation

Stephen, P.R. & Timothy, A.J. (2018, pp.108-11) suggested that self-determination theory and goal-setting theory are well supported contemporary theories of motivation, he/she is capable of performing a task. The higher , the staff self-efficiacy, the move confidence the staff has in whose ability to succed. So, in different situations, staffs with low self-efficacy are more likely to lessen whose effort. Self-efficacy can create a positive working attitude in which those ith hifh efficacy become more engaged in their tasks and then , increase performance, which increases efficacy further.
However, it brings one question: How to increase the staff's confidence to reaise whose performance? I believe that if the HR organization can provide effective training to any skillful shortage of staffs number to satisfy to different departments' efficient performnce needs. The effective training can be the best method to assist unskillful staffs to

raise whose task effort. The effective training programs can often be made use of enactive training teaching materials by choice of the most suitable teaching materials and building the confidence to staff individual skill. In fact, one reason training works is that it increases self-efficacy, particularly when the training is interactive and feedback is given from the trainees. So, the trainer can know whether every trainee feels what difficulty to understand whose feeback in every training course. Individuals with higher levels of self-efficacy also appear to bring more benefits from training programs and are more likely to use their training on the job. So, effective training teaching material arrangement and enough time feedback in every training course will be one imported factor to raise staff individual efficiency to whose goals.

2. Developing people through effective delegation skill

Delegation is one important method to raise staff individual efficiency and productive performance. In fact, it has relation to effective HR department's decision. For example, if one poor management skillful manager who is selected to employ to do the manager position in the organization's one department. If his/her managing skill is poor, he/she doesn't know how to arrange different kinds of tasks to delegate to whose department's different positions of stafss to work. If his/her judgement of arrangement task's skill is poor. He/her delegates the urgent or important tasks to one low skillful or low effort staff to attempt to do the tasks, then, it will bring raising task difficulty to the low skillful or low effort staff. He/she won't improve whose performance , even it will bring pressure to the low skillful employee to work inefficiently.

Bernard, M. B. & Bruce, J.A. (1994, pp.11-13) explained that developing people's skill, it can through delegation. Because of such influences are downsizing, restructuring and greater informational competition for products and services, organizational leaders need have rethink rapidly to know how to manage their people and organizations. With fewer employees required to share greater work loads, also many of these leaders need to raise capacity of their human resources to keep competition with rapid changes in the market.

In fact, one common way for organizations to train potential leaders to development opportunities is through rotating job assignments, often these assignment are in highly visible positions in different departments across the organization and ususally for a specified period of time. The purpose of such assignments is to test the capabilities of the leader in an attempt to improve potential, perhaps talent into actual talent. The costs of such programs, however are considerable.

However, if the HR department makes judgement to select on poor managing skillful and less mangement working experience's manager to manage whose department. He/she is the poort delegation skillful manager to know how to arrange the urgent or important tasks to whom to do. Then, the relocation expenses, salary increases, losses in efficiency an derrors during the learning process, and the cost of failure is a new assignment all contribute to the high price of development. Hence, every manager needs to learn and know how to use job rotation for development in short term or long term urgent or important tasks' finishing assignments in due dare to avoid organizational inefficient consequence occurrences or caused, due to the manager's poor delegation skill.

In fact, delegation is a way or method to solve how to deal any important or urgent tasks to be finished before due date. Defined simply, it is the assignment of responsibility or authority to another, it is a frequently used management tool in organizations aroung the world. Delegation has been conceptualized as a time management tool, a decision making process or a way of getting more things, dome through others. However, if the manager delegates one urgent or important task to one neglect or careless staff to attempt to do it. It is possible tc bring inefficiency or poor performance.

Although, delegation can ease the job og managing and increase the effectiveness of the manager, this is a relatively narrow view point of delegation. However, it is not absolent sure or guarantee to any managers can develop right or reasonable delegation or how or why some leaders seem to be able to develop the potential in others when other leaders can not . Hence, it implies that if the HR department can select the best managing skillful manager to attempt to do the position. Then, his/her wrong delegation possible occurrence chance will be reduced to the minimum level to avoid inefficiency and low productive performance causing chance to be raised to the organization.

3. Predictive analytics when the organization feels its human resources need to be changed.

The third point to raise efficiency and improve productive factor is that the organization feels need to know how it ought need to spend time and human resources to gather external environment and internal data to predict when the suddent environment changes to influence insufficient productivities and poor performance is caused from unpredictive poor environment change factor influence.

Jac, F.E & John, R.M. (2014, pp.13-16) explained that if any organizations expected they can adapt any external poor economic environment as well as organization's weakness causing changing factors to bring their organization's inefficiencies and poor productive performance causing in long term. They need to know and learn how to predict their HR needs when their HR is needed to be changed in order to adapt the sudden external economic environment changing and organization's weakness to cause its inefficiency and low productive performance consequence.

Any organization needs to gather datas concern: What will be needed to be lead potentially? What are the future market demands? What are the leader's changing managing attitude to let whole company's staffs to adapt easily in order to encourage they raise efficiency and improve productive performance more easily? It also needs to predict when the external forces drives will occue to cause how it's human resource strategy needs to be changed to adapt or fight the sudden external forces drives influence in order to avoid inefficiency or low productive performance consequence. The external force drives may include: Slow encourage growth, technological labour shortage, customer complaints number increasing, new competitors' products existing or enter the market, government regulation prohibition. Then, the organization gathers all these external environment forces drives datas to predict when these poor external environment changes will occur.

On the one hand, it can implement human resource changing strategy, such as reducing workforce, new skills needed, increasing training, focusing on service, informing employees new benfits regulations. On the other hand, it needs to change the internal drives factors, due to the external forces drives sudden change influence that it feels it needs to change its human resources strategy in order to avoid inefficiency or/and low productive performance causing.

However, it also needs to find whether its organizational internal drives factors also need to be changed to avoid inefficiency and/or poor productive performance causing. The internal drivers factors may include: Whether the company itself needs to change new company vision, due to external environment changes, whether it needs to change its leadership gap to adapt sudden external environment factors influence, whether its organizational culture and brand image and finances sources and expenditure controlling need to be changed , due to external environment changes influence factor.

However, when the organization discovers that it needs to change its human resource strategy in order to adapt the sudden economic environment poor changing influence. Then, it needs to explain to let its employees to know whether why and how and what aspects, it needs to change, how to implement accelerate development to adapt the possible sudden economic environment poor changing occurrence, when it is the right time to begin transformation, reimplement to wage/salary payment policy and evaluation performance method, due to the possible sudden poor economic environment changing influence. Hence, when the organization can predict when the external poor economic environment changes influences to cause the inefficiency and poor productive performance consequence, then it can know how to change its human resource strategy in order to adapt the possibe sudden poor economy environment changing influence to cause inefficiency and poor productive performance causing consequence in possible.

4. Good working place environment and no sex labor different treatment factor

One good working place environment is another important factor to influence employee individual performance and efficiency to be improved. I assume that selected the best skillful workers to do the tasks, but it is not represent these best skillful workers must raise efficiency to do their tasks .

Fiona, M.W, (2004, p.79) indicated one case to explain why skillful working won't be possible to raise efficiency to work , if the organization's workplace environment is poor and it implements unfair sex treatment to employ workers between male and female sex and different country. The case concerns one factory employed over 2,000 workers, women made up nearly two-thirds of these workers. Nearly, half the workers were other country, e.g. Asian. The division of labour was clear, when the Western country, e.g. US men were knitters, mechanics, dyers and top managers. The Asian women workers in the finishing process in personnel, and white collar jobs.

The finished jobs women did-were low paid, repetitive and based upon piece production, which is conceived of as a natural attribute, not a skill, they joined fabric together, bar-tasked herms, and operated button-sewing machines. An Asian woman might sew side seams all day, every day, for weeks at a time, unlikely the assembly line that controlled the flow of work, the machinist wzs dependant on the supervisor to bring work to her. This could be caused frustration to the factory's women labour. The individual worker had no control over what she would do not tried to boost her speed on each operation in order to secure the highest rate for the job. The women disliked bring moved between jobs , but management looked for flexibility in the use of their labour power.

However, the work environment was physically tiring, noisy and monotonous. This was a common response to the job . The Asian women were expected to meet targets of production each day and had to work under pressure to earn a bonus. Monotony was eased through conversation, jokes. The Asian women's work was domesticated by them. For example, the factory manager feels the female workers seem to be very machine and tells them you are my machine. So, it causes the factory Asian female workers feel angry and complain the Western , US manager's verbal joke behavior is poor to cause the Asian women workers have negative emotion to do ths factory job often.

Hence , it explains that why this factory Asian female workers won't raise efficiency in possible, due to its unfair job treatment, the factory management high level positions are selected to US male applicants to do. So, the Asian female workers will feel unfair position treatment and they feel they won't earn promotion chance, even they have effot to do any managment positions to replace these US male managers in this factory . Morevover, their factory managers' attitudes are poor to let them to feel often. The US managers often speak to them, such as my machine. They have not said high value Asian female workers to let them to feel they are important employees in this factory 's manufacturing deparment. Hence, their emotions will be influenced to be poor and spend less effort to hard to work to raise piece productivity in order to earn bonus , due to they feel tried to work , because they have no rest time in this factory. Finally, the poor working environment , it lacks good air condition facilities to let them to feel more cool feeling to comfort to work in summer or warm heater facilities to let them to feel warm feeling to comfort to work in winter. Moreover, machines' sound cause noise pollution to cause them to feel ear listening physical illness when they need to work in noisy workplace workplace in long term in possible.

All these poor psychological and physical both factors will influence the skillful Asian female workers to perform poorly. Hence, it seems this factory needs to change its employment strategy to let the Asian female workers have fair employment chance to apply the manager positions in this factory. It aims to let the Asian female workers feel they have promotion chance to promote to do any low, middle and high level of management positions and attempt to manage the Western male workers to do the hand-needed productive tasks.

This factory may arrange one training department. For example, the training department can provide factory manager's managing skillful training courses to teach the high potential Asian female workers to be promoted to do the management level positions. So, they have chance to be promoted to the high level management position from the middle level and low level management position in this factory. So, the fair position promotion , salary reward and improved factory's facilities, e.g. increasing factory spaces, increasing machine number, increasing warming heaters and air conditoners number these factory facility management issues will influence the Asian female worker individual efficiency and productive performance to be improved in possible.

However, this factory management will need to solve the most important influential poor performance or inefficiency workplace environment facilities problem in the factory, the organization must need to change in order to let these Asian female workers feel comfortable environment to work in this factory. The maintenance system to improve the factory's workplace environment to be felt more comfortable to these female workers. The type of tasks may include: Inspection for leaks in hydraulic system, predictive maintenance, scan all electrical connectons with infrared, cleaning and removing debris from machine, taking reading rcord of machine operating every day time, scheduled replacement and removing replace pump every three years, interviewing the operator to enquire how machine is operating, carrying on analysis concerns how a type of machine performance history analysis. So, these factory's facility management tasks are important factor to let these Asian female workers to feel safe to work in this factory,when this factory female workers feel this workplace environment is improved to be more safe and comfortable as well as their illnesses are reduced and promotion. Ths another review point is that many Western male manager individual behavior and attitude is changed to let them to feel better and the training course is effective to let them to feel skillful level is raised . Then, the skillful Asian female worker individual piece productive number will be raised as well as the low skillful Asian female worker individual productive performance will be improved, due to the organization has effective training courses to let them to learn how to raise their skills to produce every piece of product in efficient way.

5. How can school's human resource bring educators' teaching efficiency?

These are considered questions concern school organiations : Must school's training deparment need to be arranged? How can school organizations' human resource department help educators determine cost (efficiency) , how to define student performance (effectiveness) and how to compare cost to raise high quality of teaching performance to teachers? Has it relationship how to guide policy and allcation of resources between school organizations' human resource strategy and the structure that produce the greatest improvement to teacher individual teaching behavior for the least cost to satisfy student's learning need?

I beleive that school's human resource deparment has relationship to influence teacher individual teaching performance and student's individual performance in eduation industry. The teaching effect to teacher's performance includes: high cost and high performance or high cost and low performance or low cost and high performance or low cost and low performance.

However, these unpredictive variable factors will bring above these teaching effect to be changed, even the school's human resource department had selected the teacher who owns more years teaching experience and high level of qualification to teach the subject. It means that the high level qualification and owning more teaching experience's teacher can teach whose students in poor teaching performance to bring poor learning effectiveness to whose students. The unpredictive variable factors may include socio-economic make up of student high populations, so the prior excellent performance teacher needs to teach 30 students in one classroom in prior. Currently, he/she needs to teach 50, even more tham 50 students number in one classroom, due to the shortage of teachers number and/or increasing students number to the school , size of school, e.g. classroom number is no increasing change, but the students number is increasing to the school, teacher turnover ratio increases, it is possible that many teachers feel pressure to teach many students in one classroom. They want to change career development, they feel unfair salary and benefit treatments, they are complained by students of student's family, they feel themselves teaching studetn's learning performance, it can't improve and examinatons results are worse. They teachers concrn themselves' teaching responsibilities more than students themselves learning responsibilities as well as the mobility of students, e.g. many students often change different subjects to learn or many students are leaving this school and they change to another new school to learn. So, the teacher needs to spend much time to teach the new students , due to they are replaced to the leaving old students as well as the teacher needs to spend much time to teach the new student swhen he/she is studying this new subject and he/she is the another old subject student. So, these unpredictive variable factors will cause the owning past excellent teaching performance's teachers feel pressure to teacher his/her students currently. If any one of above these unpredictable factors influence to his/her teaching behavioral needs to be changed to in order to adapt this sudden new and complex's teaching workplace or learning environment. Then, it is possible that their teaching performance will be worse, due to they feel pressure to teach their students in classroom every day.

So, it seems that it has no relationship between the effective human resource department's application selection process and the training course' content and the teacher's teaching performance because all of above these factors can not predicted when one of them will occur in order to find solutions to solve these problems in prior. Moreover, it also explain that teacher individual teaching performance has no direct relationship to human resource department, because one excellent teaching performance teacher will have possible to be influenced his/her teaching performance to be poor, due to any on of above these factors influence.

- How can school teaching training influence to teacher individual teaching performance?

Has any school training necessary to train every teacher individual teaching skill to be raised? It depends on these factors to judge whether it is that all schools have necessary to arrange any training courses to achieve to raise whose teacher individual skill aim. These factors may include: Whether the junior or high school teacher had been trained whose teaching skill in prior of another old school, before he/she had not employed to teacher this school's students? Whether the junior or high school teacher has good teaching efficiency of career development or owning more years of teaching experience before? Whether the junior or high school teacher had attended relevant research of career development education before? Whether the fresh teacher, experience teacher, and teacher with master or above educational background, he/she has the best overall teaching efficiency of career development before? Whether the junior or high school teacher with higher teaching faith of career development, he/she will be higher teaching efficiency career development before?

Hence, any one of above factors will influence that whether the teacher must be necessary to be trained to raise the teaching skills when he/she changes to this new school to teach his/her students from another old school. Unless the teacher is one new teacher who lacks more years of teaching experience and/or lacks any training courses to be taught to prepare to develop his/her teaching career from prior another old school. It is possible that thi new teacher will face how to adapt the change of educational environment, understanding the importance of career development to teach whose students in this school. Then, this school ought spend time and effort to arrange different kinds ot training courses to re-establish the own teaching faith environment to let this new teacher to learn how to adapt whose teaching career in development in this school and keeping up to train this new teacher to learn how the teaching ethusiasm and ideal are the initial motivation to develop whose teaching career development in this school successfully. Hence, it seems that must be necessary to set up training department to any schools. If the school's all teachers who own more years of teaching experience and all they had been trained how to develop theor career in order to teach their students more understanding. Otherwise, if the school has many new teachers who lacks more years of teaching experience and they had not ever trained to develop their teaching career from other schools before. Then, this school ought set up one training department to arrange any training courses to prepare how to design different kinds of training course materials or contents to teach them in order to achieve to raise the new teachers' teaching skills more succedsfully.

Hence, it seems that education organization's training cause is only necessary to be arranged as well as the training department is also needed to set up, it is based on whether the school had how may new students number who are studying in the school.

6. Can tourism industry's human resource management influence to improve productivity in airline, travel agent, hotel tourism sectors?

In tourism industry, measuring productivity froma HRM prespective is extremely difficult and has proven to be a limitation within the tourism sector. Due to the customers are not tangible. For example, how can the travel agent measure its travel consultant individual service performance to evaluate whether the travelling customer feels or does not feel satisfactory loyalty from his/her service? How can the airline measure its pilot , airline front-line travelling passenger service attendant indiviual service performance to evaluate whether his/her travelling passenger feels or does not feel satisfactory to whose service performance?

However, the complaint number whether it is more or less to the airline or travel agent's service behavior , it does not represent whose service attitude or behavior or performance is poor absolutely because there are many travelling consumers whose complaints are unreasonable , although they feel satisfactory to the airline attendent or airline front -line service staffs individual service performance, but if they feel unhappy to be caused by the airline or travel agent service staff. They will still compain their performance. For this suitation example , it is possible that the travelling passenger is delayed to catch the airplance to fly, due to the country's sudden worse weather influnce, he/ she will complain the airline fron-line counter travelling customer service staffs, it concerns when the air plane will arrive the airport, if the airline counter service staff's feedback is that the airplane needs long time arrival. Then, the travelling passengers will complain to the airline counter service staffs in angry. But in fact, the air plane delays to arrive the airport, the airline counter service staffs ought not need responsibilitie to explain the reason why they can not assist the delayed air plane to arrive the country in easier. Furthermore, thy will be complained unreasonably. Hence, it is difficult to measure tourism sector's service staffs ' performance, also the complaint exact number is not one judgement factor to measure their service performance absolutely.

I assume any tourism industry's front -line service airline staffs, they must attempt to serve their travelling passenger in positive service attitude and behavior. So, any tourism industy, how to improve their front -line service staff performance in order to let they to know how to deal unreasonable complaints in sudden unpredictive suitation. Their training materials or contents my include: Teaching them how to provide positive feedback to treat any travelling passenger individual difficult problems or unreasonable complaints in order to reduce their psychological pressure to unknown how to treat these passenger individual related problems when they are facing in airports or travelling agent workplaces. The travelling agent or airline travelling service organizations can attempt to collect measures of employee performance from customers , for example, comment cards in hotel rooms, airplane, travel agent's workplace, mystery shoppers etc. more focus shouls be pleased on this form of evaluation. In order to evaluate the actually place value on the customer ratings to every employee. The all every day, the form of evaluation concerning the actually value on the customer ratings , will be gathered to strategic , it has how many customers feel good or bad ratings to every employee individual performance when every one's tasks are finishing. Due to one month, it can make statistic report to calculate how much performance marks to give to every employee in order to evaluate whether every one's performance is satisfactory to be accempted to the lowest level. If the employee's marks rating is low, his/her department manager can arrange a time and day to meet him/her to discuss whether which aspects of problems who feels in order to give recommendation how to improve his/her service attitude to let customer to give higher marks rating to him/her next time.

Hence tourism industry's service sector organizations need to have one training department to arrange courses how to improve employee service performance in order to let customer to give higher marks rating to very one as well as finding methods how to excite every front line service employee individual loyalty , they can increase their confidence to know how to deal sudden unreasonable complaints in effective and efficient positive attitude.

In conclusion, how to improve employee service performance issue will be any tourism service organization's HRM concerning problem. HR department needs to know how to find the most effective methods to solve how improvement of front line employee individual performance problem in order to raise the airline or travel agent's quality of service to let itself further customers to feel its service performance is better than others.

- How can HR improve public sector efficiency?

Any country's public service organizations will concern how to improve service servants' service performance in order to satisfy itself country's citizen's needs. Any public service organization's HR department needs to concern how to decentralize of political power and spend responsibility to sub-national government, arrange appropriate humwn resource management to any departments in the public education and health sector, there is evidence tht increasing the scale of operations may improve efficiency.

However, some important factors to any publis service organizations, they need to concern: thre is no one model of performance budgeting comtinue need to adapt their approach to the relevant political and or institutional content. A fixed common whole-of-government planning and reporting framework importance to any country's public service organization, every country's public service organization's HR department ought design itself government wide systems that can automatically link performance results to resource allocation should be avoided, because they may distort incentives and because it is difficult to design systems that take chance to avoid to cause of poor performance to any country's orgnization public service absolutely independent assessments of performance information should be carried out, the support of political and administratoin leaders is vital for implementation , the staff and resource capacity of the ministry of finance and spending ministries is critical, reform approaches need to be adapted to evolving circumstances . It is also important to develop incentives to motivate civil servants and politicians to change their behaviors, learning -by-doing process is important to influence every country's public service organization's success, e.g. learning to make the budget process more responsive to priorities, learning to make management, practices more flexible , such that defined priorities are easier to achieve, learning how to strengthen competitive pressures among providers of public services and where not incompatible with equity considerations, containing the demand for public services . Hence, all above of any one issues which will be public service organization's solve consideration issues if they expect public servants can raise service performance to let themselves citizens to feel in themselves countries.

In conclusion, any public or private organizations need have on effective human resource management strategy to raise employee individual performance efficiency. In summary, these several aspects, they need to consider that they many include: avoiding to lack of continuous training and education , when the organizaton's top manager feels to consider investments in itself human assets. It trends to see human expenses as something which needs to be minimised. For example, lack of continuous learning opportunities is because the organization only consider to devolve to bottom line profit award aim in short term. In general, leaders have not consider how to develop talent employees in their organizations. They have mistakenly highly consider they need to truly reward the qualities that provide for long term stability. If their organizations failure, it is due to lacking skill development is appropriate when they believe performance can be important of the employees acquire or refresh job related skills from himself/herself job related learning effort every day as well as increasing job responsibility to him/her. However, effective training arrangement can bring fresh job knowledge and learning job related practice chance to raise every employee individual confidence and skill or effort to learn whethe he/she ought need how to do himself/herself daily simply or complex tasks in right or correct attitude in order to minimize mistakes chance occurrences, even avoid mistakes occurrances again in possible . Hence, effective training courses arrangment will have necessary to some organizations,wheh they had have many new employees are working in their organizations.

Reference

Bernard, M.B. & Bruce, J. A. (1994) Improving organizational effectiveness through transformational leadership: US. Sage publications, Inc. pp. 11-13.

Fiona, M.W. (2004). organizational behavior and work , a critical introduction, 2 ed. : New York, US, Oxford university press, pp.79 .

Jac, F.E.& John , R.M. (2014) predictive analytics for HRM:US Pearson Education pp.13-16

Stephen, P.R. & Timothy, A.J. (2018). Essentials of organizational behavior, 14 ed.: US. Pearson Education, Inc. pp.108-110.

In any organizations, instead of their human resource department function includes: interview, selecting, training, peformance evaluation management, reward management etc. based human related responsibilities. Can human resource department assist any other departments to raise employee individual productivies and efficiencies? Although, it has only indirect relationship to productivity and efficiency issue. It does not represent that it can not assist any departments to attempt to raise employee individual productivity and efficiency. I shall indicate evidences to explain how it will possible occur.

How to impact human resource (HR)management on turnover productivity and corporate financial performance? I believe that HR development has an economically and statistically significant impact on both intermediate employee outcomes (turnover and productivity) and short and long term measures of corporate financial performance.

In fact, the impact of human resource management policies and practices on firm performance is an important topic in the fields of human resource management. The high performance work practices may include comprenhensive employee recruitment, selection procedures, incentive compensation and performance management system , and implementing employee engagement, training strategies, which can improve the knowledge, skills, and abilities of a firm's current and potential employees.

However, arguments made in related research are that a firm's current and potential human resources are important considerations in the development and execution of the firm's strategic plan. It brings this question: How and why organization's human resource development plan which can assist to raise employee individual productive efficiency. I shall assume that one organizational human resource policies, if it is effective, then it can bring properly contribution to provide a diect and economically significant contribution to the firm.

An organization's effective HR department development is needed to support by the development and vaidation of an instrument that reflects the system of high performance work practices adpted by the firm's employees. Then, if the organization has high performance work practices, it implies that its all employees had adopted its working environment to do every task efficiently. The reasons include as below points:

The first point, their employees must add value to the firm's production processes from effective training methods to achieve raising levels of individual performance successfully.

The second point, the skills to the firm seeks must be rare. So, the firm's employees can have rare skills to contribute to their organization to compare the other similar industry's organizations, their owning general ordinary skills of employees. So, rare skillful employees and effective training both methods which will be important factors to assist different departments to improve performance and raise productive efficiency more easily. Also, it implies that an effective Hr department will have above characteristics when the organization's human resource department owns above these competitive advantages. Then, achieving the raising productivity and efficiency aim will achieve more easily.

The third point, the human resource department needs to have long-term human capital development to invest to the firm's employees to continue to train them to improve their hard and soft both skills. Investments in human resource development, they are similar to organization's equipment or facilities investments. So, they both are such as to invest in the firm's specific human captial, which can further decrease the probability of such imitation by qualitatively differentiating between the firm's specific talent employees and the other same industry firms' employees .Thus,

it means that the firm's employees' skills and efforts will be better to compare its same industry competitors' employees, if the firm has long-term human resource talent development strategy to its different departments' employees to prepare to raise heir skills and efforts level.
The final point, a firm's human resources must not be subject to replacement by technological development, e.g. artificial intelligence, computer, information technology, internet or other substitutes of they are to provide a source of competitive advantage. Although, when the organization can choose to apply technologies investment to replace all employees or many employees to do their tasks in order to manufacture any products. However, the labor saving technological method is not suitable to half-service industry. For example, a restaurant can use robots to replace waitors to deliver food to clients to eat. It is simple food delivery tasks. But it is not good to apply robots to replace cookers to do their cooking tasks, because robot cooker's cooking skill, it is difficult to imitate human cooker's cooking skill in order to make same or similar ,even better food taste to let restaurant clients to feel better food taste. For the restaurant's cashier task example, because casher;s calculation ability will be netter to compare (AI) 's calculation ability. Human cashier's calculation error chance will be lesser to compare robot cashier's calculation skills. So , if the restaurant's all cookers, waitors and cashiers whose tasks all are replaced by robots. It will bring under utilized consequence because robots can not perform above their maximum potential more easier than human employees in the restaurant's long term working hours every day, because the restaurants employ more than one staff to prepare to replace the staff when he/she feels tired to need rest. Otherwise, these all restaurant positions , it has only one robot to do its position in the restaurant. I believe that these three cashier and cooker and waitor robots will be used to the maximum of utilization , then they will be older and calculation, walking and cooking speed and effort will also be slow and poor when they are used long hours every day to serve clients in the restaurant.
Thus, when one service organization, it can not only concentrate on robots to replace human employees to do their positions' all tasks. It will perform worse than the service organizaion , it only uses robots to replace some employees to do some tasks and some positions still use human employees to do themselves tasks. Otherwise, one manufacturing organization, e.g. car manufacturing organization, it may apply robots to participate some part of human employees' manufacturing tasks in the car manufacturing process. It will help human empoyees to manufacturing can productivities and efficiencies more than the another car manufacturing firm only employs human workers to manufacture all cars in car manufacturing process every day. When the later car manufacturing neglects to apply robots to participate the whole car manufacturing process to assist human workers to manufacture cars. Then, the later only applying human workers' car manufacturing firm which will have worse productivities and inefficiencies to compare the prior car manufacturing firm to apply both robots and human workers to manufacture any kinds of cars in whole car manufacturing process. The reason is because human workers must feel tried when they need concentrate their nevous to manufacture many cars every day. If robots can participate their car manufacturing tasks to share work load to assist they to finish some more difficult or complex part of tasks, then they will feel less nervous and they reduce pressure to manufacture the complex part of car manufacturing process. Then, their efficiency and productive performance will be raised in possible.

● Can HRM practice influence employee individual skills through the HR development of a firm's human capitals in organization?

It will need long time to implement HR development in any organization, if the organization decides to implement long term HR development strategy, e.g. it can provide formal and informal training experiences, such as basic skills training, on-the-job experience, coaching, mentoring, and managemet development can further influence employee individual skills to be improved in other to achieve raising productive efficiency to every department.

Other raising productivity and efficient method is that employee psychological method. The HRM practices can attempt to encourage employees themselves motivates to work both harder and smarter. So, when some employees have higher skills, they can do tasks more better , but these igher skillful employees limit their effort to work in lazy. So, their productive efficiency can not achieve the best performance. The question is concerned how to persuade or encourage them to motivate and perform work hard? The solution may be performance appraisals that assess individual or work group performance, linking these appraisals to incentive compensation systems, the use of internal promotion systems that can focus on employee merit, e.g. the performance evaluation may have three levels:excellent performance, good performance and poor performance three levels. Thus, the oftenhigh performance employees can earn more reward to compensate their efforts or promote them to higher positions in short time in order to persuade how they perform their tasks to improve their productivities and efficiencies in short time.

The another raising productive efficient method is to change organizational culture to be better. It seems that organizational culture can influence turnove. I shall assume that it has relationship between productivity and organizational culture. For example, if the organization's culture or policy is not one punishment method. Then, it can enourage the lazy workers to apply many leaving pay holidays and the lazy workers will be encouraged to absence and the absenteeism number will increase. It needs to change its traditional organizational culture in order to threaten the lazy employees need to hard to work. When the firm changes punishment method to treat these often absent employees, then these lazy workers number will be possible to reduce, due to they do not want be punished. When the organization has punishment method and disciplinary actions to treat the employees who have higher absenteeism, due to they feel afraid to be punished. Thus, the positive consequencey may be increasingly product quality and direct labor efficiency, lower absenteeism, and labor high teams increased productivity.

In conclusion, it seems that when one organization can achieve to implement one long term human resource management development strategy to its any departmental employees, it have more chance to bring long term raising productivities and efficiencies and improving employee individual behavioral performance consequence.

● Human resource raising productive
efficient factors

Why some organizations' productive efficiency can be improved? Otherwise, why some organizations' productive efficiency can not be improved? Does it has relationship between the organization's efficiency and effective human

resource (HR) strategy? I shall indicated some cases to explain why it is possible that an ineffective HR department strategy which will influence inefficiency and low productive performance to the organization in long term.
How to achieve efficienct organizational behavior, it depends on many factors. However, effective training can raise employee individual efficiency, due to the effective training can raise the employee individual confidence to do whose task.

1.0 Effective training preparation

Stephen, P.R. & Timothy, A.J. (2018, pp.108-11) suggested that self-determination theory and goal-setting theory are well supported contemporary theories of motivation, he/she is capable of performing a task. The higher , the staff self-efficiacy, the move confidence the staff has in whose ability to succed. So, in different situations, staffs with low self-efficacy are more likely to lessen whose effort. Self-efficacy can create a positive working attitude in which those ith hifh efficacy become more engaged in their tasks and then , increase performance, which increases efficacy further.
However, it brings one question: How to increase the staff's confidence to reaise whose performance? I believe that if the HR organization can provide effective training to any skillful shortage of staffs number to satisfy to different departments' efficient performnce needs. The effective training can be the best method to assist unskillful staffs to raise whose task effort. The effective training programs can often be made use of enactive training teaching materials by choice of the most suitable teaching materials and building the confidence to staff individual skill. In fact, one reason training works is that it increases self-efficacy, particularly when the training is interactive and feedback is given from the trainees. So, the trainer can know whether every trainee feels what difficulty to understand whose feeback in every training course. Individuals with higher levels of self-efficacy also appear to bring more benefits from training programs and are more likely to use their training on the job. So, effective training teaching material arrangement and enough time feedback in every training course will be one imported factor to raise staff individual efficiency to whose goals.

2. Developing people through effective delegation skill

Delegation is one important method to raise staff individual efficiency and productive performance. In fact, it has relation to effective HR department's decision. For example, if one poor management skillful manager who is selected to employ to do the manager position in the organization's one department. If his/her managing skill is poor, he/she doesn't know how to arrange different kinds of tasks to delegate to whose department's different positions of stafss to work. If his/her judgement of arrangement task's skill is poor. He/her delegates the urgent or important tasks to one low skillful or low effort staff to attempt to do the tasks, then, it will bring raising task difficulty to the low skillful or low effort staff. He/she won't improve whose performance , even it will bring pressure to the low skillful employee to work inefficiently.
Bernard, M. B. & Bruce, J.A. (1994, pp.11-13) explained that developing people's skill, it can through delegation. Because of such influences are downsizing, restructuring and greater informational competition for products and services, organizational leaders need have rethink rapidly to know how to manage their people and organizations.

With fewer employees required to share greater work loads, also many of these leaders need to raise capacity of their human resources to keep competition with rapid changes in the market.

In fact, one common way for organizations to train potential leaders to development opportunities is through rotating job assignments, often these assignment are in highly visible positions in different departments across the organization and ususally for a specified period of time. The purpose of such assignments is to test the capabilities of the leader in an attempt to improve potential, perhaps talent into actual talent. The costs of such programs, however are considerable.

However, if the HR department makes judgement to select on poor managing skillful and less mangement working experience's manager to manage whose department. He/she is the poort delegation skillful manager to know how to arrange the urgent or important tasks to whom to do. Then, the relocation expenses, salary increases, losses in efficiency an derrors during the learning process, and the cost of failure is a new assignment all contribute to the high price of development. Hence, every manager needs to learn and know how to use job rotation for development in short term or long term urgent or important tasks' finishing assignments in due dare to avoid organizational inefficient consequence occurrences or caused, due to the manager's poor delegation skill.

In fact, delegation is a way or method to solve how to deal any important or urgent tasks to be finished before due date. Defined simply, it is the assignment of responsibility or authority to another, it is a frequently used management tool in organizations aroung the world. Delegation has been conceptualized as a time management tool, a decision making process or a way of getting more things, dome through others. However, if the manager delegates one urgent or important task to one neglect or careless staff to attempt to do it. It is possible to bring inefficiency or poor performance.

Although, delegation can ease the job og managing and increase the effectiveness of the manager, this is a relatively narrow view point of delegation. However, it is not absolent sure or guarantee to any managers can develop right or reasonable delegation or how or why some leaders seem to be able to develop the potential in others when other leaders can not . Hence, it implies that if the HR department can select the best managing skillful manager to attempt to do the position. Then, his/her wrong delegation possible occurrence chance will be reduced to the minimum level to avoid inefficiency and low productive performance causing chance to be raised to the organization.

3. Predictive analytics when the organization feels its human resources need to be changed.

The third point to raise efficiency and improve productive factor is that the organization feels need to know how it ought need to spend time and human resources to gather external environment and internal data to predict when the suddent environment changes to influence insufficient productivities and poor performance is caused from unpredictive poor environment change factor influence.

Jac, F.E & John, R.M. (2014, pp.13-16) explained that if any organizations expected they can adapt any external poor economic environment as well as organization's weakness causing changing factors to bring their organization's inefficiencies and poor productive performance causing in long term. They need to know and learn how to predict their HR needs when their HR is needed to be changed in order to adapt the sudden external economic environment changing and organization's weakness to cause its inefficiency and low productive performance consequence.

Any organization needs to gather datas concern: What will be needed to be lead potentially? What are the future market demands? What are the leader's changing managing attitude to let whole company's staffs to adapt easily in order to encourage they raise efficiency and improve productive performance more easily? It also needs to predict when the external forces drives will occue to cause how it's human resource strategy needs to be changed to adapt or fight the sudden external forces drives influence in order to avoid inefficiency or low productive performance consequence. The external force drives may include: Slow encourage growth, technological labour shortage, customer complaints number increasing, new competitors' products existing or enter the market, government regulation prohibition. Then, the organization gathers all these external environment forces drives datas to predict when these poor external environment changes will occur.

On the one hand, it can implement human resource changing strategy, such as reducing workforce, new skills needed, increasing training, focusing on service, informing employees new benfits regulations. On the other hand, it needs to change the internal drives factors, due to the external forces drives sudden change influence that it feels it needs to change its human resources strategy in order to avoid inefficiency or/and low productive performance causing. However, it also needs to find whether its organizational internal drives factors also need to be changed to avoid inefficiency and/or poor productive performance causing. The internal drivers factors may include: Whether the company itself needs to change new company vision, due to external environment changes, whether it needs to change its leadership gap to adapt sudden external environment factors influence, whether its organizational culture and brand image and finances sources and expenditure controlling need to be changed , due to external environment changes influence factor.

However, when the organization discovers that it needs to change its human resource strategy in order to adapt the sudden economic environment poor changing influence. Then, it needs to explain to let its employees to know whether why and how and what aspects, it needs to change, how to implement accelerate development to adapt the possible sudden economic environment poor changing occurrence, when it is the right time to begin transformation, reimplement to wage/salary payment policy and evaluation performance method, due to the possible sudden poor economic environment changing influence. Hence, when the organization can predict when the external poor economic environment changes influences to cause the inefficiency and poor productive performance consequence, then it can know how to change its human resource strategy in order to adapt the possibe sudden poor economy environment changing influence to cause inefficiency and poor productive performance causing consequence in possible.

4. Good working place environment and no sex labor different treatment factor

One good working place environment is another important factor to influence employee individual performance and efficiency to be improved. I assume that selected the best skillful workers to do the tasks, but it is not represent these best skillful workers must raise efficiency to do their tasks .

Fiona, M.W, (2004, p.79) indicated one case to explain why skillful working won't be possible to raise efficiency to work , if the organization's workplace environment is poor and it implements unfair sex treatment to employ workers between male and female sex and different country. The case concerns one factory employed over 2,000 workers, women made up nearly two-thirds of these workers. Nearly, half the workers were other country, e.g. Asian. The division of labour was clear, when the Western country, e.g. US men were knitters, mechanics, dyers and top managers. The Asian women workers in the finishing process in personnel, and white collar jobs.

The finished jobs women did-were low paid, repetitive and based upon piece production, which is conceived of as a natural attribute, not a skill, they joined fabric together, bar-tasked herms, and operated button-sewing machines. An Asian woman might sew side seams all day, every day, for weeks at a time, unlikely the assembly line that controlled the flow of work, the machinist wzs dependant on the supervisor to bring work to her. This could be caused frustration to the factory's women labour. The individual worker had no control over what she would do not tried to boost her speed on each operation in order to secure the highest rate for the job. The women disliked bring moved between jobs , but management looked for flexibility in the use of their labour power.

However, the work environment was physically tiring, noisy and monotonous. This was a common response to the job . The Asian women were expected to meet targets of production each day and had to work under pressure to earn a bonus. Monotony was eased through conversation, jokes. The Asian women's work was domesticated by them. For example, the factory manager feels the female workers seem to be very machine and tells them you are my machine. So, it causes the factory Asian female workers feel angry and complain the Western , US manager's verbal joke behavior is poor to cause the Asian women workers have negative emotion to do ths factory job often.

Hence , it explains that why this factory Asian female workers won't raise efficiency in possible, due to its unfair job treatment, the factory management high level positions are selected to US male applicants to do. So, the Asian female workers will feel unfair position treatment and they feel they won't earn promotion chance, even they have effot to do any managment positions to replace these US male managers in this factory . Morevover, their factory managers' attitudes are poor to let them to feel often. The US managers often speak to them, such as my machine. They have not said high value Asian female workers to let them to feel they are important employees in this factory 's manufacturing deparment. Hence, their emotions will be influenced to be poor and spend less effort to hard to work to raise piece productivity in order to earn bonus , due to they feel tried to work , because they have no rest time in this factory. Finally, the poor working environment , it lacks good air condition facilities to let them to feel more cool feeling to comfort to work in summer or warm heater facilities to let them to feel warm feeling to comfort to work in winter. Moreover, machines' sound cause noise pollution to cause them to feel ear listening physical illness when they need to work in noisy workplace workplace in long term in possible.

All these poor psychological and physical both factors will influence the skillful Asian female workers to perform poorly. Hence, it seems this factory needs to change its employment strategy to let the Asian female workers have fair employment chance to apply the manager positions in this factory. It aims to let the Asian female workers feel they have promotion chance to promote to do any low, middle and high level of management positions and attempt to manage the Western male workers to do the hand-needed productive tasks.

This factory may arrange one training department. For example, the training department can provide factory manager's managing skillful training courses to teach the high potential Asian female workers to be promoted to do the management level positions. So, they have chance to be promoted to the high level management position from the middle level and low level management position in this factory. So, the fair position promotion , salary reward and improved factory's facilities, e.g. increasing factory spaces, increasing machine number, increasing warming heaters and air conditoners number these factory facility management issues will influence the Asian female worker individual efficiency and productive performance to be improved in possible.

However, this factory management will need to solve the most important influential poor performance or inefficiency workplace environment facilities problem in the factory, the organization must need to change in order to let these Asian female workers feel comfortable environment to work in this factory. The maintenance system to improve the factory's workplace environment to be felt more comfortable to these female workers. The type of tasks may include: Inspection for leaks in hydraulic system, predictive maintenance, scan all electrical connectons with infrared, cleaning and removing debris from machine, taking reading rcord of machine operating every day time, scheduled replacement and removing replace pump every three years, interviewing the operator to enquire how machine is operating, carrying on analysis concerns how a type of machine performance history analysis. So, these factory's facility management tasks are important factor to let these Asian female workers to feel safe to work in this factory,when this factory female workers feel this workplace environment is improved to be more safe and comfortable as well as their illnesses are reduced and promotion. Ths another review point is that many Western male manager individual behavior and attitude is changed to let them to feel better and the training course is effective to let them to feel skillful level is raised . Then, the skillful Asian female worker individual piece productive number will be raised as well as the low skillful Asian female worker individual productive performance will be improved, due to the organization has effective training courses to let them to learn how to raise their skills to produce every piece of product in efficient way.

5. How can school's human resource bring educators‘ teaching efficiency?

These are considered questions concern school organiations : Must school's training deparment need to be arranged? How can school organizations' human resource department help educators determine cost (efficiency) , how to define student performance (effectiveness) and how to compare cost to raise high quality of teaching performance to teachers? Has it relationship how to guide policy and allcation of resources between school organizations‘ human resource strategy and the structure that produce the greatest improvement to teacher individual teaching behavior for the least cost to satisfy student's learning need?

I beleive that school's human resource deparment has relationship to influence teacher individual teaching performance and student's individual performance in eduation industry. The teaching effect to teacher's performance includes: high cost and high performance or high cost and low performance or low cost and high performance or low cost and low performance.

However, these unpredictive variable factors will bring above these teaching effect to be changed, even the school's human resource department had selected the teacher who owns more years teaching experience and high level of qualification to teach the subject. It means that the high level qualification and owning more teaching experience's teacher can teach whose students in poor teaching performance to bring poor learning effectiveness to whose students. The unpredictive variable factors may include socio-economic make up of student high populations, so the prior excellent performance teacher needs to teach 30 students in one classroom in prior. Currently, he/she needs to teach 50, even more tham 50 students number in one classroom, due to the shortage of teachers number and/or increasing students number to the school , size of school, e.g. classroom number is no increasing change, but the students number is increasing to the school, teacher turnover ratio increases, it is possible that many teachers feel pressure to teach many students in one classroom. They want to change career development, they feel unfair salary and benefit treatments, they are complained by students of student's family, they feel themselves teaching studetn's learning performance, it can't improve and examinatons results are worse. They teachers concrn themselves' teaching responsibilities more than students themselves learning responsibilities as well as the mobility of students, e.g. many students often change different subjects to learn or many students are leaving this school and they change to another new school to learn. So, the teacher needs to spend much time to teach the new students , due to they are replaced to the leaving old students as well as the teacher needs to spend much time to teach the new student swhen he/she is studying this new subject and he/she is the another old subject student. So, these unpredictive variable factors will cause the owning past excellent teaching performance's teachers feel pressure to teacher his/her students currently. If any one of above these unpredictable factors influence to his/her teaching behavioral needs to be changed to in order to adapt this sudden new and complex's teaching workplace or learning environment. Then, it is possible that their teaching performance will be worse, due to they feel pressure to teach their students in classroom every day.

So, it seems that it has no relationship between the effective human resource department's application selection process and the training course' content and the teacher's teaching performance because all of above these factors can not predicted when one of them will occur in order to find solutions to solve these problems in prior. Moreover, it also explain that teacher individual teaching performance has no direct relationship to human resource department, because one excellent teaching performance teacher will have possible to be influenced his/her teaching performance to be poor, due to any on of above these factors influence.

- How can school teaching training influence to teacher individual teaching performance?

Has any school training necessary to train every teacher individual teaching skill to be raised? It depends on these factors to judge whether it is that all schools have necessary to arrange any training courses to achieve to raise whose teacher individual skill aim. These factors may include: Whether the junior or high school teacher had been trained whose teaching skill in prior of another old school, before he/she had not employed to teacher this school's students? Whether the junior or high school teacher has good teaching efficiency of career development or owning more years of teaching experience before? Whether the junior or high school teacher had attended relevant research of career development education before? Whether the fresh teacher, experience teacher, and teacher with master or above educational background, he/she has the best overall teaching efficiency of career development before? Whether the junior or high school teacher with higher teaching faith of career development, he/she will be higher teaching efficiency career development before?

Hence, any one of above factors will influence that whether the teacher must be necessary to be trained to raise the teaching skills when he/she changes to this new school to teach his/her students from another old school. Unless the teacher is one new teacher who lacks more years of teaching experience and/or lacks any training courses to be taught to prepare to develop his/her teaching career from prior another old school. It is possible that thi new teacher will face how to adapt the change of educational environment, understanding the importance of career development to teach whose students in this school. Then, this school ought spend time and effort to arrange different kinds ot training courses to re-establish the own teaching faith environment to let this new teacher to learn how to adapt whose teaching career in development in this school and keeping up to train this new teacher to learn how the teaching ethusiasm and ideal are the initial motivation to develop whose teaching career development in this school successfully. Hence, it seems that must be necessary to set up training department to any schools. If the school's all teachers who own more years of teaching experience and all they had been trained how to develop theor career in order to teach their students more understanding. Otherwise, if the school has many new teachers who lacks more years of teaching experience and they had not ever trained to develop their teaching career from other schools before. Then, this school ought set up one training department to arrange any training courses to prepare how to design different kinds of training course materials or contents to teach them in order to achieve to raise the new teachers' teaching skills more succedsfully.

Hence, it seems that education organization's training cause is only necessary to be arranged as well as the training department is also needed to set up, it is based on whether the school had how may new students number who are studying in the school.

6. Can tourism industry's human resource management influence to improve productivity in airline, travel agent, hotel tourism sectors?

In tourism industry, measuring productivity froma HRM prespective is extremely difficult and has proven to be a limitation within the tourism sector. Due to the customers are not tangible. For example, how can the travel agent measure its travel consultant individual service performance to evaluate whether the travelling customer feels or does not feel satisfactory loyalty from his/her service? How can the airline measure its pilot , airline front-line travelling passenger service attendant indiviual service performance to evaluate whether his/her travelling passenger feels or does not feel satisfactory to whose service performance?

However, the complaint number whether it is more or less to the airline or travel agent's service behavior , it does not represent whose service attitude or behavior or performance is poor absolutely because there are many travelling consumers whose complaints are unreasonable , although they feel satisfactory to the airline attendent or airline front -line service staffs individual service performance, but if they feel unhappy to be caused by the airline or travel agent service staff. They will still compain their performance. For this suitation example , it is possible that the travelling passenger is delayed to catch the airplance to fly, due to the country's sudden worse weather influnce, he/ she will complain the airline fron-line counter travelling customer service staffs, it concerns when the air plane will arrive the airport, if the airline counter service staff's feedback is that the airplane needs long time arrival. Then, the travelling passengers will complain to the airline counter service staffs in angry. But in fact, the air plane delays to arrive the airport, the airline counter service staffs ought not need responsibilitie to explain the reason why they can not assist the delayed air plane to arrive the country in easier. Furthermore, thy will be complained unreasonably. Hence, it is difficult to measure tourism sector's service staffs ' performance, also the complaint exact number is not one judgement factor to measure their service performance absolutely.

I assume any tourism industry's front -line service airline staffs, they must attempt to serve their travelling passenger in positive service attitude and behavior. So, any tourism industy, how to improve their front -line service staff performance in order to let they to know how to deal unreasonable complaints in sudden unpredictive suitation. Their training materials or contents my include: Teaching them how to provide positive feedback to treat any travelling passenger individual difficult problems or unreasonable complaints in order to reduce their psychological pressure to unknown how to treat these passenger individual related problems when they are facing in airports or travelling agent workplaces. The travelling agent or airline travelling service organizations can attempt to collect measures of employee performance from customers , for example, comment cards in hotel rooms, airplane, travel agent's workplace, mystery shoppers etc. more focus shouls be pleased on this form of evaluation. In order to evaluate the actually place value on the customer ratings to every employee. The all every day, the form of evaluation concerning the actually value on the customer ratings , will be gathered to strategic , it has how many customers feel good or bad ratings to every employee individual performance when every one's tasks are finishing. Due to one month, it can make statistic report to calculate how much performance marks to give to every employee in order to evaluate whether every one's performance is satisfactory to be accempted to the lowest level. If the employee's marks rating is low, his/her department manager can arrange a time and day to meet him/her to discuss whether which aspects of problems who feels in order to give recommendation how to improve his/her service attitude to let customer to give higher marks rating to him/her next time.

Hence tourism industry's service sector organizations need to have one training department to arrange courses how to improve employee service performance in order to let customer to give higher marks rating to very one as well as finding methods how to excite every front line service employee individual loyalty , they can increase their confidence to know how to deal sudden unreasonable complaints in effective and efficient positive attitude.

In conclusion, how to improve employee service performance issue will be any tourism service organization's HRM concerning problem. HR department needs to know how to find the most effective methods to solve how improvement of front line employee individual performance problem in order to raise the airline or travel agent's quality of service to let itself further customers to feel its service performance is better than others.

● How can HR improve public sector efficiency?

Any country's public service organizations will concern how to improve service servants' service performance in order to satisfy itself country's citizen's needs. Any public service organization's HR department needs to concern how to decentralize of political power and spend responsibility to sub-national government, arrange appropriate humwn resource management to any departments in the public education and health sector, there is evidence tht increasing the scale of operations may improve efficiency.

However, some important factors to any publis service organizations, they need to concern: thre is no one model of performance budgeting comtinue need to adapt their approach to the relevant political and or institutional content. A fixed common whole-of-government planning and reporting framework importance to any country's public service organization, every country's public service organization's HR department ought design itself government wide systems that can automatically link performance results to resource allocation should be avoided, because they may distort incentives and because it is difficult to design systems that take chance to avoid to cause of poor performance to any country's orgnization public service absolutely independent assessments of performance information should be carried out, the support of political and administratoin leaders is vital for implementation , the staff and resource capacity of the ministry of finance and spending ministries is critical, reform approaches need to be adapted to evolving circumstances . It is also important to develop incentives to motivate civil servants and politicians to change their behaviors, learning -by-doing process is important to influence every country's public service organization's success, e.g. learning to make the budget process more responsive to priorities, learning to make management, practices more flexible , such that defined priorities are easier to achieve, learning how to strengthen competitive pressures among providers of public services and where not incompatible with equity considerations, containing the demand for public services . Hence, all above of any one issues which will be public service organization's solve consideration issues if they expect public servants can raise service performance to let themselves citizens to feel in themselves countries.

In conclusion, any public or private organizations need have on effective human resource management strategy to raise employee individual performance efficiency. In summary, these several aspects, they need to consider that they many include: avoiding to lack of continuous training and education , when the organizaton's top manager feels to consider investments in itself human assets. It trends to see human expenses as something which needs to be minimised. For example, lack of continuous learning opportunities is because the organization only consider to devolve to bottom line profit award aim in short term. In general, leaders have not consider how to develop talent employees in their organizations. They have mistakenly highly consider they need to truly reward the qualities that provide for long term stability. If their organizations failure, it is due to lacking skill development is appropriate when they believe performance can be important of the employees acquire or refresh job related skills from himself/herself job related learning effort every day as well as increasing job responsibility to him/her. However, effective training arrangement can bring fresh job knowledge and learning job related practice chance to raise every employee individual confidence and skill or effort to learn whethe he/she ought need how to do himself/herself daily simply or complex tasks in right or correct attitude in order to minimize mistakes chance occurrences, even avoid mistakes occurrances again in possible . Hence, effective training courses arrangment will have necessary to some organizations,wheh they had have many new employees are working in their organizations.

Reference

Bernard, M.B. & Bruce, J. A. (1994) Improving organizational effectiveness through transformational leadership: US. Sage publications, Inc. pp. 11-13.

Fiona, M.W. (2004). organizational behavior and work , a critical introduction, 2 ed. : New York, US, Oxford university press, pp.79 .

Jac, F.E.& John , R.M. (2014) predictive analytics for HRM:US Pearson Education pp.13-16

Stephen, P.R. & Timothy, A.J. (2018). Essentials of organizational behavior, 14 ed.: US. Pearson Education, Inc. pp.108-110.

In any organizations, instead of their human resource department function includes: interview, selecting, training, peformance evaluation management, reward management etc. based human related responsibilities. Can human resource department assist any other departments to raise employee individual prcductivies and efficiencies? Although, it has only indirect relationship to productivity and efficiency issue. It does not represent that it can not assist any departments to attempt to raise employee individual productivity and efficiency. I shall indicate evidences to explain how it will possible occur.

How to impact human resource (HR)management on turnover productivity and corporate financial performance? I believe that HR development has an economically and statistically significant impact on both intermediate employee outcomes (turnover and productivity) and short and long term measures of corporate financial performance.

In fact, the impact of human resource management policies and practices on firm performance is an important topic in the fields of human resource management. The high performance work practices may include comprenhensive employee recruitment, selection procedures, incentive compensation and performance management system , and implementing employee engagement, training strategies, which can improve the knowledge, skills, and abilities of a firm's current and potential employees.

However, arguments made in related research are that a firm's current and potential human resources are important considerations in the development and execution of the firm's strategic plan. It brings this question: How and why organization's human resource development plan which can assist to raise employee individual productive efficiency. I shall assume that one organizational human resource policies, if it is effective, then it can bring properly contribution to provide a diect and economically significant contribution to the firm.

An organization's effective HR department development is needed to support by the development and vaidation of an instrument that reflects the system of high performance work practices adpted by the firm's employees. Then, if the organization has high performance work practices, it implies that its all employees had adopted its working environment to do every task efficiently. The reasons include as below points:

The first point, their employees must add value to the firm's production processes from effective training methods to achieve raising levels of individual performance successfully.

The second point, the skills to the firm seeks must be rare. So, the firm's employees can have rare skills to contribute to their organization to compare the other similar industry's organizations, their owning general ordinary skills of employees. So, rare skillful employees and effective training both methods which will be important factors to assist different departments to improve performance and raise productive efficiency more easily. Also, it implies that an effective Hr department will have above characteristics when the organization's human resource department owns above these competitive advantages. Then, achieving the raising productivity and efficiency aim will achieve more easily.

The third point, the human resource department needs to have long-term human capital development to invest to the firm's employees to continue to train them to improve their hard and soft both skills. Investments in human resource development, they are similar to organization's equipment or facilities investments. So, they both are such as to invest in the firm's specific human captial, which can further decrease the probability of such imitation by qualitatively differentiating between the firm's specific talent employees and the other same industry firms‘ employees .Thus, it means that the firm's employees' skills and efforts will be better to compare its same industry competitors‘ employees, if the firm has long-term human resource talent development strategy to its different departments' employees to prepare to raise heir skills and efforts level.

The final point, a firm's human resources must not be subject to replacement by technological development, e.g. artificial intelligence, computer, information technology, internet or other substitutes of they are to provide a source of competitive advantage. Although, when the organization can choose to apply technologies investment to replace all employees or many employees to do their tasks in order to manufacture any products. However, the labor saving technological method is not suitable to half-service industry. For example, a restaurant can use robots to replace waitors to deliver food to clients to eat. It is simple food delivery tasks. But it is not good to apply robots to replace cookers to do their cooking tasks, because robot cooker's cooking skill, it is difficult to imitate human cooker's cooking skill in order to make same or similar ,even better food taste to let restaurant clients to feel better food taste. For the restaurant's cashier task example, because casher;s calculation ability will be netter to compare (AI) 's calculation ability. Human cashier's calculation error chance will be lesser to compare robot cashier's calculation skills. So , if the restaurant's all cookers, waitors and cashiers whose tasks all are replaced by robots. It will bring under utilized consequence because robots can not perform above their maximum potential more easier than human employees in the restaurant's long term working hours every day, because the restaurants employ more than one staff to prepare to replace the staff when he/she feels tired to need rest. Otherwise, these all restaurant positions , it has only one robot to do its position in the restaurant. I believe that these three cashier and cooker and waitor robots will be used to the maximum of utilization , then they will be older and calculation, walking and cooking speed and effort will also be slow and poor when they are used long hours every day to serve clients in the restaurant.

Thus, when one service organization, it can not only concentrate on robots to replace human employees to do their positions' all tasks. It will perform worse than the service organizaion , it only uses robots to replace some employees to do some tasks and some positions still use human employees to do themselves tasks. Otherwise, one manufacturing organization, e.g. car manufacturing organization, it may apply robots to participate some part of human employees' manufacturing tasks in the car manufacturing process. It will help human empoyees to manufacturing can productivities and efficiencies more than the another car manufacturing firm only employs human workers to manufacture all cars in car manufacturing process every day. When the later car manufacturing neglects to apply robots to participate the whole car manufacturing process to assist human workers to manufacture cars. Then, the later only applying human workers' car manufacturing firm which will have worse productivities and inefficiencies to compare the prior car manufacturing firm to apply both robots and human workers to manufacture any kinds of cars in whole car manufacturing process. The reason is because human workers must feel tried when they need concentrate their nevous to manufacture many cars every day. If robots can participate their car manufacturing tasks to share work load to assist they to finish some more difficult or complex part of tasks, then they will feel less nervous and they reduce pressure to manufacture the complex part of car manufacturing process. Then, their efficiency and productive performance will be raised in possible.

- Can HRM practice influence employee individual skills through the HR development of a firm's human capitals in organization?

It will need long time to implement HR development in any organization, if the organization decides to implement long term HR development strategy, e.g. it can provide formal and informal training experiences, such as basic skills training, on-the-job experience, coaching, mentoring, and managemet development can further influence employee individual skills to be improved in other to achieve raising productive efficiency to every department.

Other raising productivity and efficient method is that employee psychological method. The HRM practices can attempt to encourage employees themselves motivates to work both harder and smarter. So, when some employees have higher skills, they can do tasks more better , but these igher skillful employees limit their effort to work in lazy. So, their productive efficiency can not achieve the best performance. The question is concerned how to persuade or encourage them to motivate and perform work hard? The solution may be performance appraisals that assess individual or work group performance, linking these appraisals to incentive compensation systems, the use of internal promotion systems that can focus on employee merit, e.g. the performance evaluation may have three levels:excellent performance, good performance and poor performance three levels. Thus, the oftenhigh performance employees can earn more reward to compensate their efforts or promote them to higher positions in short time in order to persuade how they perform their tasks to improve their productivities and efficiencies in short time.

The another raising productive efficient method is to change organizational culture to be better. It seems that organizational culture can influence turnove. I shall assume that it has relationship between productivity and organizational culture. For example, if the organization's culture or policy is not one punishment method. Then,

it can enourage the lazy workers to apply many leaving pay holidays and the lazy workers will be encouraged to absence and the absenteeism number will increase. It needs to change its traditional organizational culture in order to threaten the lazy employees need to hard to work. When the firm changes punishment method to treat these often absent employees, then these lazy workers number will be possible to reduce, due to they do not want be punished. When the organization has punishment method and disciplinary actions to treat the employees who have higher absenteeism, due to they feel afraid to be punished. Thus, the positive consequencey may be increasingly product quality and direct labor efficiency, lower absenteeism, and labor high teams increased productivity.
In conclusion, it seems that when one organization can achieve to implement one long term human resource management development strategy to its any departmental employees, it have more chance to bring long term raising productivities and efficiencies and improving employee individual behavioral performance consequence.

● Human resource raising productive
efficient factors

Why some organizations' productive efficiency can be improved? Otherwise, why some organizations' productive efficiency can not be improved? Does it has relationship between the organization's efficiency and effective human resource (HR) strategy? I shall indicated some cases to explain why it is possible that an ineffective HR department strategy which will influence inefficiency and low productive performance to the organization in long term.
How to achieve efficienct organizational behavior, it depends on many factors. However, effective training can raise employee individual efficiency, due to the effective training can raise the employee individual confidence to do whose task.

1.0 Effective training preparation
Stephen, P.R. & Timothy, A.J. (2018, pp.108-11) suggested that self-determination theory and goal-setting theory are well supported contemporary theories of motivation, he/she is capable of performing a task. The higher , the staff self-efficiacy, the move confidence the staff has in whose ability to succed. So, in different situations, staffs with low self-efficacy are more likely to lessen whose effort. Self-efficacy can create a positive working attitude in which those ith hifh efficacy become more engaged in their tasks and then , increase performance, which increases efficacy further.
However, it brings one question: How to increase the staff's confidence to reaise whose performance? I believe that if the HR organization can provide effective training to any skillful shortage of staffs number to satisfy to different departments' efficient performnce needs. The effective training can be the best method to assist unskillful staffs to raise whose task effort. The effective training programs can often be made use of enactive training teaching materials by choice of the most suitable teaching materials and building the confidence to staff individual skill. In fact, one reason training works is that it increases self-efficacy, particularly when the training is interactive and feedback is given from the trainees. So, the trainer can know whether every trainee feels what difficulty to understand whose feeback in every training course. Individuals with higher levels of self-efficacy also appear to bring more benefits

from training programs and are more likely to use their training on the job. So, effective training teaching material arrangement and enough time feedback in every training course will be one imported factor to raise staff individual efficiency to whose goals.

2. Developing people through effective delegation skill

Delegation is one important method to raise staff individual efficiency and productive performance. In fact, it has relation to effective HR department's decision. For example, if one poor management skillful manager who is selected to employ to do the manager position in the organization's one department. If his/her managing skill is poor, he/she doesn't know how to arrange different kinds of tasks to delegate to whose department's different positions of stafss to work. If his/her judgement of arrangement task's skill is poor. He/her delegates the urgent or important tasks to one low skillful or low effort staff to attempt to do the tasks, then, it will bring raising task difficulty to the low skillful or low effort staff. He/she won't improve whose performance , even it will bring pressure to the low skillful employee to work inefficiently.

Bernard, M. B. & Bruce, J.A. (1994, pp.11-13) explained that developing people's skill, it can through delegation. Because of such influences are downsizing, restructuring and greater informational competition for products and services, organizational leaders need have rethink rapidly to know how to manage their people and organizations. With fewer employees required to share greater work loads, also many of these leaders need to raise capacity of their human resources to keep competition with rapid changes in the market.

In fact, one common way for organizations to train potential leaders to development opportunities is through rotating job assignments, often these assignment are in highly visible positions in different departments across the organization and ususally for a specified period of time. The purpose of such assignments is to test the capabilities of the leader in an attempt to improve potential, perhaps talent into actual talent. The costs of such programs, however are considerable.

However, if the HR department makes judgement to select on poor managing skillful and less mangement working experience's manager to manage whose department. He/she is the poort delegation skillful manager to know how to arrange the urgent or important tasks to whom to do. Then, the relocation expenses, salary increases, losses in efficiency an derrors during the learning process, and the cost of failure is a new assignment all contribute to the high price of development. Hence, every manager needs to learn and know how to use job rotation for development in short term or long term urgent or important tasks' finishing assignments in due dare to avoid organizational inefficient consequence occurrences or caused, due to the manager's poor delegation skill.

In fact, delegation is a way or method to solve how to deal any important or urgent tasks to be finished before due date. Defined simply, it is the assignment of responsibility or authority to another, it is a frequently used management tool in organizations aroung the world. Delegation has been conceptualized as a time management tool, a decision making process or a way of getting more things, dome through others. However, if the manager delegates one urgent or important task to one neglect or careless staff to attempt to do it. It is possible to bring inefficiency or poor performance.

Although, delegation can ease the job og managing and increase the effectiveness of the manager, this is a relatively narrow view point of delegation. However, it is not absolent sure or guarantee to any managers can develop right or reasonable delegation or how or why some leaders seem to be able to develop the potential in others when other leaders can not . Hence, it implies that if the HR department can select the best managing skillful manager to attempt to do the position. Then, his/her wrong delegation possible occurrence chance will be reduced to the minimum level to avoid inefficiency and low productive performance causing chance to be raised to the organization.

3. Predictive analytics when the organization feels its human resources need to be changed.

The third point to raise efficiency and improve productive factor is that the organization feels need to know how it ought need to spend time and human resources to gather external environment and internal data to predict when the suddent environment changes to influence insufficient productivities and poor performance is caused from unpredictive poor environment change factor influence.

Jac, F.E & John, R.M. (2014, pp.13-16) explained that if any organizations expected they can adapt any external poor economic environment as well as organization's weakness causing changing factors to bring their organization's inefficiencies and poor productive performance causing in long term. They need to know and learn how to predict their HR needs when their HR is needed to be changed in order to adapt the sudden external economic environment changing and organization's weakness to cause its inefficiency and low productive performance consequence.

Any organization needs to gather datas concern: What will be needed to be lead potentially? What are the future market demands? What are the leader's changing managing attitude to let whole company's staffs to adapt easily in order to encourage they raise efficiency and improve productive performance more easily? It also needs to predict when the external forces drives will occue to cause how it's human resource strategy needs to be changed to adapt or fight the sudden external forces drives influence in order to avoid inefficiency or low productive performance consequence. The external force drives may include: Slow encourage growth, technological labour shortage, customer complaints number increasing, new competitors' products existing or enter the market, government regulation prohibition. Then, the organization gathers all these external environment forces drives datas to predict when these poor external environment changes will occur.

On the one hand, it can implement human resource changing strategy, such as reducing workforce, new skills needed, increasing training, focusing on service, informing employees new benfits regulations. On the other hand, it needs to change the internal drives factors, due to the external forces drives sudden change influence that it feels it needs to change its human resources strategy in order to avoid inefficiency or/and low productive performance causing. However, it also needs to find whether its organizational internal drives factors also need to be changed to avoid inefficiency and/or poor productive performance causing. The internal drivers factors may include: Whether the company itself needs to change new company vision, due to external environment changes, whether it needs to change its leadership gap to adapt sudden external environment factors influence, whether its organizational culture and brand image and finances sources and expenditure controlling need to be changed , due to external environment

changes influence factor.
However, when the organization discovers that it needs to change its human resource strategy in order to adapt the sudden economic environment poor changing influence. Then, it needs to explain to let its employees to know whether why and how and what aspects, it needs to change, how to implement accelerate development to adapt the possible sudden economic environment poor changing occurrence, when it is the right time to begin transformation, reimplement to wage/salary payment policy and evaluation performance method, due to the possible sudden poor economic environment changing influence. Hence, when the organization can predict when the external poor economic environment changes influences to cause the inefficiency and poor productive performance consequence, then it can know how to change its human resource strategy in order to adapt the possibe sudden poor economy environment changing influence to cause inefficiency and poor productive performance causing consequence in possible.

4. Good working place environment and no sex labor different treatment factor

One good working place environment is another important factor to influence employee individual performance and efficiency to be improved. I assume that selected the best skillful workers to do the tasks, but it is not represent these best skillful workers must raise efficiency to do their tasks .
Fiona, M.W, (2004, p.79) indicated one case to explain why skillful working won't be possible to raise efficiency to work , if the organization's workplace environment is poor and it implements unfair sex treatment to employ workers between male and female sex and different country. The case concerns one factory employed over 2,000 workers, women made up nearly two-thirds of these workers. Nearly, half the workers were other country, e.g. Asian. The division of labour was clear, when the Western country, e.g. US men were knitters, mechanics, dyers and top managers. The Asian women workers in the finishing process in personnel, and white collar jobs.
The finished jobs women did-were low paid, repetitive and based upon piece production, which is conceived of as a natural attribute, not a skill, they joined fabric together, bar-tasked herms, and operated button-sewing machines. An Asian woman might sew side seams all day, every day, for weeks at a time, unlikely the assembly line that controlled the flow of work, the machinist wzs dependant on the supervisor to bring work to her. This could be caused frustration to the factory's women labour. The individual worker had no control over what she would do not tried to boost her speed on each operation in order to secure the highest rate for the job. The women disliked bring moved between jobs , but management looked for flexibility in the use of their labour power.
However, the work environment was physically tiring, noisy and monotonous. This was a common response to the job . The Asian women were expected to meet targets of production each day and had to work under pressure to earn a bonus. Monotony was eased through conversation, jokes. The Asian women's work was domesticated by them. For example, the factory manager feels the female workers seem to be very machine and tells them you are my machine. So, it causes the factory Asian female workers feel angry and complain the Western , US manager's verbal joke behavior is poor to cause the Asian women workers have negative emotion to do ths factory job often.
Hence , it explains that why this factory Asian female workers won't raise efficiency in possible, due to its unfair

job treatment, the factory management high level positions are selected to US male applicants to do. So, the Asian female workers will feel unfair position treatment and they feel they won't earn promotion chance, even they have effot to do any managment positions to replace these US male managers in this factory . Morevover, their factory managers' attitudes are poor to let them to feel often. The US managers often speak to them, such as my machine. They have not said high value Asian female workers to let them to feel they are important employees in this factory 's manufacturing deparment. Hence, their emotions will be influenced to be poor and spend less effort to hard to work to raise piece productivity in order to earn bonus , due to they feel tried to work , because they have no rest time in this factory. Finally, the poor working environment , it lacks good air condition facilities to let them to feel more cool feeling to comfort to work in summer or warm heater facilities to let them to feel warm feeling to comfort to work in winter. Moreover, machines' sound cause noise pollution to cause them to feel ear listening physical illness when they need to work in noisy workplace workplace in long term in possible.

All these poor psychological and physical both factors will influence the skillful Asian female workers to perform poorly. Hence, it seems this factory needs to change its employment strategy to let the Asian female workers have fair employment chance to apply the manager positions in this factory. It aims to let the Asian female workers feel they have promotion chance to promote to do any low, middle and high level of management positions and attempt to manage the Western male workers to do the hand-needed productive tasks.

This factory may arrange one training department. For example, the training department can provide factory manager's managing skillful training courses to teach the high potential Asian female workers to be promoted to do the management level positions. So, they have chance to be promoted to the high level management position from the middle level and low level management position in this factory. So, the fair position promotion , salary reward and improved factory's facilities, e.g. increasing factory spaces, increasing machine number, increasing warming heaters and air conditoners number these factory facility management issues will influence the Asian female worker individual efficiency and productive performance to be improved in possible.

However, this factory management will need to solve the most important influential poor performance or inefficiency workplace environment facilities problem in the factory, the organization must need to change in order to let these Asian female workers feel comfortable environment to work in this factory. The maintenance system to improve the factory's workplace environment to be felt more comfortable to these female workers. The type of tasks may include: Inspection for leaks in hydraulic system, predictive maintenance, scan all electrical connectons with infrared, cleaning and removing debris from machine, taking reading rcord of machine operating every day time, scheduled replacement and removing replace pump every three years, interviewing the operator to enquire how machine is operating, carrying on analysis concerns how a type of machine performance history analysis. So, these factory's facility management tasks are important factor to let these Asian female workers to feel safe to work in this factory,when this factory female workers feel this workplace environment is improved to be more safe and comfortable as well as their illnesses are reduced and promotion. Ths another review point is that many Western male manager individual behavior and attitude is changed to let them to feel better and the training course is effective to let them to feel skillful level is raised . Then, the skillful Asian female worker individual piece productive number will be raised as well as the low skillful Asian female worker individual productive performance will be improved, due to the organization has effective training courses to let them to learn how to raise their skills to produce every piece of product in efficient way.

5. How can school's human resource bring educators' teaching efficiency?

These are considered questions concern school organiations : Must school's training deparment need to be arranged? How can school organizations' human resource department help educators determine cost (efficiency) , how to define student performance (effectiveness) and how to compare cost to raise high quality of teaching performance to teachers? Has it relationship how to guide policy and allcation of resources between school organizations' human resource strategy and the structure that produce the greatest improvement to teacher individual teaching behavior for the least cost to satisfy student's learning need?

I beleive that school's human resource deparment has relationship to influence teacher individual teaching performance and student's individual performance in eduation industry. The teaching effect to teacher's performance includes: high cost and high performance or high cost and low performance or low cost and high performance or low cost and low performance.

However, these unpredictive variable factors will bring above these teaching effect to be changed, even the school's human resource department had selected the teacher who owns more years teaching experience and high level of qualification to teach the subject. It means that the high level qualification and owning more teaching experience's teacher can teach whose students in poor teaching performance to bring poor learning effectiveness to whose students. The unpredictive variable factors may include socio-economic make up of student high populations, so the prior excellent performance teacher needs to teach 30 students in one classroom in prior. Currently, he/she needs to teach 50, even more tham 50 students number in one classroom, due to the shortage of teachers number and/or increasing students number to the school , size of school, e.g. classroom number is no increasing change, but the students number is increasing to the school, teacher turnover ratio increases, it is possible that many teachers feel pressure to teach many students in one classroom. They want to change career development, they feel unfair salary and benefit treatments, they are complained by students of student's family, they feel themselves teaching studetn's learning performance, it can't improve and examinatons results are worse. They teachers concrn themselves' teaching responsibilities more than students themselves learning responsibilities as well as the mobility of students, e.g. many students often change different subjects to learn or many students are leaving this school and they change to another new school to learn. So, the teacher needs to spend much time to teach the new students , due to they are replaced to the leaving old students as well as the teacher needs to spend much time to teach the new student swhen he/she is studying this new subject and he/she is the another old subject student. So, these unpredictive variable factors will cause the owning past excellent teaching performance's teachers feel pressure to teacher his/her students currently. If any one of above these unpredictable factors infuence to his/her teaching behavioral needs to be changed to in order to adapt this sudden new and complex's teaching workplace or learning environment. Then, it is possible that their teaching performance will be worse, due to they feel pressure to teach their students in classroom every day.

So, it seems that it has no relationship between the effective human resource department's application selection process and the training course' content and the teacher's teaching performance because all of above these factors can not predicted when one of them will occur in order to find solutions to solve these problems in prior. Moreover, it also explain that teacher individual teaching performance has no direct relationship to human resource department, because one excellent teaching performance teacher will have possible to be influenced his/her teaching performance to be poor, due to any on of above these factors influence.

- How can school teaching training influence to teacher individual teaching performance?

Has any school training necessary to train every teacher individual teaching skill to be raised? It depends on these factors to judge whether it is that all schools have necessary to arrange any training courses to achieve to raise whose teacher individual skill aim. These factors may include: Whether the junior or high school teacher had been trained whose teaching skill in prior of another old school, before he/she had not employed to teacher this school's students? Whether the junior or high school teacher has good teaching efficiency of career development or owning more years of teaching experience before? Whether the junior or high school teacher had attended relevant research of career development education before? Whether the fresh teacher, experience teacher, and teacher with master or above educational background, he/she has the best overall teaching efficiency of career development before? Whether the junior or high school teacher with higher teaching faith of career development, he/she will be higher teaching efficiency career development before?

Hence, any one of above factors will influence that whether the teacher must be necessary to be trained to raise the teaching skills when he/she changes to this new school to teach his/her students from another old school. Unless the teacher is one new teacher who lacks more years of teaching experience and/or lacks any training courses to be taught to prepare to develop his/her teaching career from prior another old school. It is possible that thi new teacher will face how to adapt the change of educational environment, understanding the importance of career development to teach whose students in this school. Then, this school ought spend time and effort to arrange different kinds ot training courses to re-establish the own teaching faith environment to let this new teacher to learn how to adapt whose teaching career in development in this school and keeping up to train this new teacher to learn how the teaching ethusiasm and ideal are the initial motivation to develop whose teaching career development in this school successfully. Hence, it seems that must be necessary to set up training department to any schools. If the school's all teachers who own more years of teaching experience and all they had been trained how to develop theor career in order to teach their students more understanding. Otherwise, if the school has many new teachers who lacks more years of teaching experience and they had not ever trained to develop their teaching career from other schools before. Then, this school ought set up one training department to arrange any training courses to prepare how to design different kinds of training course materials or contents to teach them in order to achieve to raise the new teachers' teaching skills more succedsfully.

Hence, it seems that education organization's training cause is only necessary to be arranged as well as the training department is also needed to set up, it is based on whether the school had how may new students number who are studying in the school.

6. Can tourism industry's human resource management influence to improve productivity in airline, travel agent, hotel tourism sectors?

In tourism industry, measuring productivity froma HRM prespective is extremely difficult and has proven to be a limitation within the tourism sector. Due to the customers are not tangible. For example, how can the travel agent measure its travel consultant individual service performance to evaluate whether the travelling customer feels or does not feel satisfactory loyalty from his/her service? How can the airline measure its pilot , airline front-line travelling passenger service attendant indiviual service performance to evaluate whether his/her travelling passenger feels or does not feel satisfactory to whose service performance?

However, the complaint number whether it is more or less to the airline or travel agent's service behavior , it does not represent whose service attitude or behavior or performance is poor absolutely because there are many travelling consumers whose complaints are unreasonable , although they feel satisfactory to the airline attendent or airline front -line service staffs individual service performance, but if they feel unhappy to be caused by the airline or travel agent service staff. They will still compain their performance. For this suitation example , it is possible that the travelling passenger is delayed to catch the airplance to fly, due to the country's sudden worse weather influnce, he/she will complain the airline fron-line counter travelling customer service staffs, it concerns when the air plane will arrive the airport, if the airline counter service staff's feedback is that the airplane needs long time arrival. Then, the travelling passengers will complain to the airline counter service staffs in angry. But in fact, the air plane delays to arrive the airport, the airline counter service staffs ought not need responsibilitie to explain the reason why they can not assist the delayed air plane to arrive the country in easier. Furthermore, thy will be complained unreasonably. Hence, it is difficult to measure tourism sector's service staffs ' performance, also the complaint exact number is not one judgement factor to measure their service performance absolutely.

I assume any tourism industry's front -line service airline staffs, they must attempt to serve their travelling passenger in positive service attitude and behavior. So, any tourism industy, how to improve their front -line service staff performance in order to let they to know how to deal unreasonable complaints in sudden unpredictive suitation. Their training materials or contents my include: Teaching them how to provide positive feedback to treat any travelling passenger individual difficult problems or unreasonable complaints in order to reduce their psychological pressure to unknown how to treat these passenger individual related problems when they are facing in airports or travelling agent workplaces. The travelling agent or airline travelling service organizations can attempt to collect measures of employee performance from customers , for example, comment cards in hotel rooms, airplane, travel agent's workplace, mystery shoppers etc. more focus shouls be pleased on this form of evaluation. In order to evaluate the actually place value on the customer ratings to every employee. The all every day, the form of evaluation concerning the actually value on the customer ratings , will be gathered to strategic , it has how many customers feel good or bad ratings to every employee individual performance when every one's tasks are finishing. Due to one month, it can make statistic report to calculate how much performance marks to give to every employee in order to evaluate whether every one's performance is satisfactory to be accempted to the lowest level. If the employee's marks rating is low, his/her department manager can arrange a time and day to meet him/her to discuss whether which aspects of problems who feels in order to give recommendation how to improve his/her service attitude to let customer to give higher marks rating to him/her next time.

Hence tourism industry's service sector organizations need to have one training department to arrange courses how to improve employee service performance in order to let customer to give higher marks rating to very one as well as finding methods how to excite every front line service employee individual loyalty , they can increase their confidence to know how to deal sudden unreasonable complaints in effective and efficient positive attitude.

In conclusion, how to improve employee service performance issue will be any tourism service organization's HRM concerning problem. HR department needs to know how to find the most effective methods to solve how improvement of front line employee individual performance problem in order to raise the airline or travel agent's quality of service to let itself further customers to feel its service performance is better than others.

- How can HR improve public sector efficiency?

Any country's public service organizations will concern how to improve service servants' service performance in order to satisfy itself country's citizen's needs. Any public service organization's HR department needs to concern how to decentralize of political power and spend responsibility to sub-national government, arrange appropriate humwn resource management to any departments in the public education and health sector, there is evidence tht increasing the scale of operations may improve efficiency.

However, some important factors to any publis service organizations, they need to concern: thre is no one model of performance budgeting comtinue need to adapt their approach to the relevant political and or institutional content. A fixed common whole-of-government planning and reporting framework importance to any country's public service organization, every country's public service organization's HR department ought design itself government wide systems that can automatically link performance results to resource allocation should be avoided, because they may distort incentives and because it is difficult to design systems that take chance to avoid to cause of poor performance to any country's orgnization public service absolutely independent assessments of performance information should be carried out, the support of political and administratoin leaders is vital for implementation , the staff and resource capacity of the ministry of finance and spending ministries is critical, reform approaches need to be adapted to evolving circumstances . It is also important to develop incentives to motivate civil servants and politicians to change their behaviors, learning -by-doing process is important to influence every country's public service organization's success, e.g. learning to make the budget process more responsive to priorities, learning to make management, practices more flexible , such that defined priorities are easier to achieve, learning how to strengthen competitive pressures among providers of public services and where not incompatible with equity considerations, containing the demand for public services . Hence, all above of any one issues which will be public service organization's solve consideration issues if they expect public servants can raise service performance to let themselves citizens to feel in themselves countries.

In conclusion, any public or private organizations need have on effective human resource management strategy to raise employee individual performance efficiency. In summary, these several aspects, they need to consider that they many include: avoiding to lack of continuous training and education , when the organizaton's top manager feels to consider investments in itself human assets. It trends to see human expenses as something which needs to be minimised. For example, lack of continuous learning opportunities is because the organization only consider to devolve to bottom line profit award aim in short term. In general, leaders have not consider how to develop talent employees in their organizations. They have mistakenly highly consider they need to truly reward the qualities that provide for long term stability. If their organizations failure, it is due to lacking skill development is appropriate when they believe performance can be important of the employees acquire or refresh job related skills from himself/herself job related learning effort every day as well as increasing job responsibility to him/her. However, effective training arrangement can bring fresh job knowledge and learning job related practice chance to raise every employee individual confidence and skill or effort to learn whethe he/she ought need how to do himself/herself daily simply or complex tasks in right or correct attitude in order to minimize mistakes chance occurrences, even avoid mistakes occurrances again in possible . Hence, effective training courses arrangment will have necessary to some organizations,wheh they had have many new employees are working in their organizations.

Reference

Bernard, M.B. & Bruce, J. A. (1994) Improving organizational effectiveness through transformational leadership: US. Sage publications, Inc. pp. 11-13.

Fiona, M.W. (2004). organizational behavior and work , a critical introduction, 2 ed. : New York, US, Oxford university press, pp.79 .

Jac, F.E.& John , R.M. (2014) predictive analytics for HRM:US Pearson Education pp.13-16

Stephen, P.R. & Timothy, A.J. (2018). Essentials of organizational behavior, 14 ed.: US. Pearson Education, Inc. pp.108-110.

9 798886 843651

Printed by Libri Plureos GmbH in Hamburg,
Germany